A PEDAGOGY OF QUESTIONING

Gerardo Ivan Hannel, Esq.

ivan@apoq.org

A PEDAGOGY OF QUESTIONING

apoq.org
ivan@apoq.org
602.710.7573

K12 Workshops
2942 N 24th Street
Suite 114-721
Phoenix, AZ 85016

ISBN 978-1491020982

First Printing, 2011

Printed in the United States of America, Phoenix, AZ

Special Thanks to

Erica Nicole Tillman for artwork and design.

CONTENTS

INTRODUCTION

This book used to be known as "Highly Effective Questioning: Challenging the Culture of Disengagement" from 1996-2011 and before that as "Cognitive Education Methodology for Teaching Content, K-12."

In 2011, I rechristened it as "A Pedagogy for Questioning" (APOQ) because that's what it fundamentally is: a detailed description of cognitive and behavioral strategies classroom teachers can practically employ to improve their in-class questioning. I teach a workshop based on this book, so as you read this book, you'll also be learning many of the ideas discussed in the workshop. I am also a trial lawyer in Phoenix, Arizona, but more on that in the final chapter of the book, where I try to connect questioning to broader ideas, like democracy and freedom. But that's many pages down the road.

Please note that readers from around the world have helped me improve this book from one edition to the next, so if you spot errors or simply want to make a suggestion, go ahead and send me an email, and I'll make every effort to incorporate corrections into future editions.

Also, before you read any further, please understand that I'm not attempting to write a textbook here. It's intended to be more of a conversation between me, and you, the reader. It is not intended as some sort of carefully worded argument of all things questioning. If there's some hyperbole or off-the-cuff remarks, or wistful remembrances, please understand that they go part and parcel with the journey that led me, and now you, to this book.

Why Pedagogy?

But before we delve into this self-described pedagogy of questioning, I think it's important to consider for a moment why pedagogy—how we teach--should itself be the focus of our attention as educators.

For at least the last 20 years, when people have discussed education reform, they often seem to have conflated improving teaching with changing "what" is taught more so than the "how" the classroom teacher actually teaches. Perhaps the hope had been that new content delivery systems (e.g., whiteboards to online courses) would by their very nature also change the pedagogy of the humans doing the teaching. Or more truthfully, perhaps it's simply easier to change objects and networks and written frameworks than to actually change people, e.g., teachers. This book, oppositely, is intended to focus very specifically on "how" one teaches, albeit just in the context of classroom questioning.

An Inconvenient Question

One of the more interesting starting points for any discussion of questioning is to ignore it entirely, and focus instead on a different question: Why aren't more students learning already? That's a puzzling question! Because there has been one revolution that would seem to have vastly accelerated learning but hasn't had the predicted effect. The Internet has made access to content or information via the Internet is now almost universal, nearly free, and essentially instantaneous yet the effect on learning has been mostly marginal for too many K-12 students—the majority, I'd say. It's like those stories where you hear someone won the lottery and then you find they are penniless a few years later. How does that happen, you wonder?

If your memory or age allows, take a moment to revisit the pre-Internet or nascent Internet period of the late 1980s and early 1990s. By today's standards, very basic computers were in schools, but because they were quite expensive, they were often organized into clusters so that small groups of students could have access to them for short periods of time. You'd go visit these clusters on your 6th rotating period or something. Depending on your age, you may remember big clusters of boxy beige plastic and bulbous glass monitors.

The information on these mostly stand-alone computers was limited to what was loaded on each of them. A student might insert an encyclopedia on a DVD (if it wasn't scratched) to increase the repository of information. But there was no information superhighway or even an information dirt road (unless you are thinking 28.8 baud modems) to get more information.

Then, the Internet really arrived. In the subsequent decade, say from 1995 to 2005, computers were initially networked within schools and eventually connected to the Internet as a whole. By 2000, some students were given laptops to take home, a "laptop for every child." Notes, lectures and even whole classes were then put online. Perhaps we were reasonable to think, "This is going to change everything!"

It is now mid 2016 at the re-writing of the latest edition of this book. Devices like the iPad put the entire world of content within the immediate grasp of the learner. The physical weight of books themselves may soon become a memory—goodbye, bookstore, my old friend. The Library of Alexandria and the Library of Congress and all the information that has been preserved in the world since written history now lights up our faces with a pale light. It's like magic.

Now go back and compare this information bounty to what a student would have had available in 1985. The library's "card catalog" might have been the student's best resource for learning new information. There was no "Internet" and no Google, no YouTube, no email, and no Facebook, Twitter, Instagram, Snapchat, et cetera. As a diligent student, if your textbook's explanation of a concept or problem wasn't very good, you were essentially stuck staring at those same few pages to divine some understanding. You couldn't pull up a video or email a friend--or the teacher--to help you. As I like to say in workshops, just not too long ago, our universe of information in the classroom was limited to just the people and things in the room with us—but no longer.

Again, in retrospect, given this incredible change in access to information, one might have reasonably assumed that learning would have skyrocketed. If information back then was equal to X, and it was going to become (X*1000), then you'd naturally expect learning to just leap off the charts. Surely, today's students use the Internet to facilitate their learning, no question. But reality hasn't conformed to our great expectations for a learning revolution as a function of the information revolution—at least in school. So the question is: where did the missing learning go?

This is a surprising outcome. Consider that even a couple of hundred years ago, if you wanted to show students an image of something, someone would have had to go sketch it on a leather canvas and bring that drawing back to you on a horse, and if they brought it back at night, you'd have to light a candle to see it. Learning was understandably difficult because information was itself scarce, costly, and delayed.

What we may infer from all this, I think, is that access to content (aka, "technology") or even frameworks encompassing content, which have been so much the focus of the last twenty or thirty years of education-reform, don't mean too much to those students who simply don't like to learn or don't know how or both. Learning is a function of access to information, but even more so a function of both the student's desire to learn and the teacher's ability to actually communicate and teach.

Let's be clear. I am no modern day Luddite. I am extremely grateful for my own access to content via the Internet or whatever comes next. I absolutely love technology. I appreciate that such technology and information will set many students free in their minds.

But for most American students, robust access to content or living under the Common Core or whatever framework comes next is not enough. Our kids need to be purposefully engaged in the act of learning—whether over the Internet or 10 feet away. Properly done, questioning strategies are a powerful means of creating that engagement. Thus, we as educators should revisit pedagogy—how we teach—in part to fulfill the new (or old) promise held out to us by information technology.

What This Book Is

This book is a set of practical strategies to help any interested reader understand the behavioral and cognitive components of effective questioning so that students will embrace the incredible access to content that is already here, and likely forthcoming. It forms a pedagogy of questioning.

Asking questions puts the learning proposition directly back on the student: Do you want to learn? Do you know how to learn? Questioning also provides the student a model for learning; we learn by asking ourselves questions, consciously or subconsciously.

The ultimate goal of this book isn't for the teacher to stream questions at students for the rest of their lives. With the teacher's help, the goal is for students to internalize a model of questions that they may ask themselves when presented with new information, new things.

It also hopes to create more and better moments of directed conversation in the classroom, more interest and energy and more thinking generally. Perhaps it can even revitalize us as adults in our teaching, too, for parts of the day. Seeing students learn by questioning is rewarding, and it's simply fun to use questions as a way of figuring out how the student comes to see his or her world, or book, or formula, or test question, or whatever.

This is not the only method of asking questions that exists nor would I make any claims beyond what I've seen personally and what I've heard from teachers who have used it themselves. They find it improves the way they ask questions and helps to increase learning. You are free to add, subtract or modify the strategies as you see fit. Take what is useful and use your own skill to adapt it to your content, your students, your environment or what have you. If something works for you, use it, and if not, discard or amend it.

I hope you find these strategies useful to your teaching, and I welcome your communication with me. My email is ivan@apoq.org or call 602-710-7573.

HISTORY

I include in this book a history of how this pedagogy came to be developed. Why include a history? First, it is important to understand that the strategies herein were developed over a long period of time, so it's not something of purely recent invention. The underlying ideas been thought about for a long time and continue to be developed. Second, and unfortunately, teachers are often told to learn some new teaching strategy and the rationale given to them is often a simple parable that goes along the lines of "one school in the middle of nowhere went from low performing to high performing just by doing something really easy. Why can't we do that, too?" I wonder if these superficial exhortations end up discrediting many good educational ideas as mere fads and inadvertently engender skepticism rather than enthusiasm to try new things. I want you, the reader, to know the history so you can sense where this all comes from and see the possibilities.

This book traces its origins to the ideas of my parents, Dr. Iles Lee Hannel and Dr. Maria Veronica Hannel and to the man who inspired them, Dr. Reuven Feuerstein of Israel. The story is a bit long, but worth it, I think.

Dr. Reuven Feuerstein

I learned about Dr. Feuerstein's background mostly from what my parents told me, though I did meet him on a few occasions in the early 1980s. Dr. Feuerstein came to Arizona and New Mexico to work with various Native American tribes, and my parents were his initial trainers in the Southwest throughout the 1980s.

Dr. Feuerstein was an observant Jew, a psychologist, a medical doctor and an educator. Relevant to educators, in the 1960s, Dr. Feuerstein was a graduate student of Dr. Jean Piaget in Geneva, who called Dr. Feuerstein a "genius," which seems about right to me. In addition to his other accomplishments, Dr. Feuerstein spoke nine languages.

My mother, originally from Guadalajara, Mexico was always a person with a pioneering mindset. She left the convent in Mexico in order to become educated in the United States, since in the 1960s women did not have a great professional role to play in Mexico. She initially went to college at UCLA, where she met my dad and they both left to attend graduate school at Vanderbilt University to become psychologists.

My mother first learned about Dr. Feuerstein when she saw a poster advertising a conference that Dr. Feuerstein was giving in Toronto, Canada. My parents lived in graduate housing and were quite poor, but managed to save enough money for my mother to fly to Toronto and learn about Dr. Feuerstein's thinking-skills program called "Instrumental Enrichment" and his learning theory called the "Mediated Learning Experience." After attending, she convinced my dad that they had to dedicate themselves to spreading Dr. Feuerstein's ideas to educators wherever they could.

I met Dr. Feuerstein on a few occasions in the 1980s when I was in middle school in Phoenix, Arizona, my hometown. I recall him having a huge white beard and looking quite like I imagined Moses might have looked. I remember my parents buying kosher foods for a conference Dr. Feuerstein was holding in Arizona, but he couldn't be convinced that the food was properly prepared under religious law. It was a bit puzzling to me, as I didn't understand why the great doctor wouldn't eat. Meeting this wizard-looking, accented sage in the reservations of the Southwest was fairly surreal, as I look back on it.

Dr. Feuerstein was born in 1921 in Eastern Europe and, according to what I can recall being told, was a survivor of the Holocaust. At some point in the 1940s, Dr. Feuerstein immigrated to the newly formed state of Israel. He was appointed as the director of the Israeli government organization (Youth Alliyah) that was responsible for helping the children and youth who had been through the Holocaust and were now in Israel to adjust and succeed in school.

Almost immediately, Dr. Feuerstein noticed many students who were not doing as well as expected. He understood that the Holocaust experience left many Jewish children without traditional familial and cultural structures. They had missed was he called the "cultural transmission" of basic norms of thinking.

Importantly, Dr. Feuerstein recognized that it would not be possible for students who had missed many years of school while escaping the Holocaust (or even just coming to a new country with a new language) to simply be placed in grade and continue on as if nothing had happened. The missing years of school and cultural transmission became a structural deficit for these students both emotionally and cognitively. Dr. Feuerstein wondered what could be done to help these children.

Concepts and Cognitive Functions

Dr. Feuerstein proposed to teach students the things he felt were prerequisite to understanding content and becoming intelligent. Dr. Feuerstein believed intelligence was actually a combination of the development of certain discrete cognitive skills plus a deep understanding of certain important concepts that radiate throughout our lives.

It is important to note that Dr. Feuerstein was firmly in favor of teaching actual "content" (e.g., facts and information); there is no critical thinking without the content about which to actually think. But he felt that school often incorrectly equated "information" with learning or thinking or intelligence. In essence, Dr. Feuerstein wanted to create an "intelligence program" that would complement normal instruction in traditional school materials.

Dr. Feuerstein created a battery of materials, really a thinking-skills curriculum to teach concepts like orientation in space, sequences, family, time and position. His curriculum also developed cognitive skills like comparison, inference, labeling, prediction and so on. If you have ever seen an IQ test, it would be as if you were to make a curriculum out of those types of materials, something that scaffolds, where each successive page is a greater cognitive challenge or higher level example of a concept. He called his program "Instrumental Enrichment."

To understand the importance of concepts and cognitive functions towards intelligence, take a moment to consider the student who has a very tenuous grasp of the concept of "time." So he or she is likely to be late, yes, but it's going to affect that student in more fundamental ways. History, as a series of related events over time becomes meaningless. A decade isn't much different than a century. Science, which takes many measurements over time, is hard to understand or connect with. The student's use of the vocabulary of time sounds tinny, something happened "then" or "before" or "later." This time-less student lives mostly in the now, not doing much planning for the next semester, the dimly apprehended time of "college" or "a career."

The student who isn't adept with cognitive act of comparison may intuitively see or know things as different, but not know how to describe those differences in any articulable way. They go to a movie and their main reflection is, "It was cool." Why? "I liked it." When confronted with where they want to live, what school they want to attend (or how to pay for it!), what should be done in some situation, they often will say "I don't know" because, sadly, they actually don't know. They have no relative measures for their own reality.

So this young person, if we combine both of these sad deficits, lives in a very here and now world, with likes and dislikes, but that's about it. I imagine them as if their field of vision were limited to just what's right in front of them, and everything else a blur.

Mediated Learning Experience

The key characteristic about Dr. Feuerstein's Instrumental Enrichment was his focus on purposefully engendering what he called "mediated learning experiences" (MLE) between teacher and learner. Specifically, his materials tried to create a mandatory interplay between the teacher and student wherein conversation, modeling and other purposeful exchanges of understanding were continuously required and designed into the materials. Dr. Feuerstein described the MLE as a purposeful, intergenerational exchange of knowledge created by an adult mediator (read: teacher) and a learner. Amongst the first publications or articles I ever read in the field of education was a pamphlet Dr. Feuerstein wrote titled "Intergenerational Cultural Transfer." I knew right then and there that I was reading something remarkable.

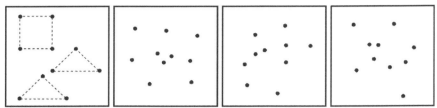

Sample Task – Spontaneous comparison of projected figure to the model.

Looking at his materials, one would notice that Dr. Feuerstein went so far as to leave out the instructions on how to complete the tasks on a page. There were few, if any, written directions on what to do. Instead, teachers had to figure out how to get students to infer the task at hand from examples or models at the top of the page, thereby creating a sort of artificial demand for these mediated learning experiences. The teacher could not simply give or read the instructions directly to the student; there were none to give. Dr. Feuerstein tried to build-in mechanisms to require mediation into his thinking-skills curriculum.

In the example above from a unit called "Orientation in Space," or often simply as "the dots," there is a model given on the left. This unit taught the skills of comparison and concepts like shapes, line segments, overlapping figures, rotation and so on. Notice there are no specific instructions provided. The question is, how could you teach this task to students. The easiest way might simply be to model the task by going to the next frame and showing how the figures are completed, drawing the lines out. However, that process of modeling requires mostly just observation from the student and so the degree of mediation would be relatively low.

A different way to teach this task would be to ask an extended series of questions. The initial question would cue for labeling behavior. What do you see in the first frame? Can you identify the shapes? What are they made up of? How many times is each dot used? The next questions might cue for inference or comparison. Are the number of dots the same in each frame? Are they in the same place as in the first frame? What can you infer happens to the shapes, if the dots are in different places? Thereafter, questions for organizing, ordering, or summarizing the task could be asked. How will you approach solving each frame? Can you summarize the task at hand? Which figure will you start looking for first, and why? What order works best?

Direct Learning v. Mediated Learning

Though I don't think he intended it at the time, Dr. Feuerstein's emphasis on mediated learning experiences could be said to have contrasted with a different diagnosis about what was thought to inhibit learning, a point of view that that some educators take even now. This is the belief that underachieving students mostly lack exposure to information generally, what Dr. Feuerstein labeled as a lack of "direct learning" experiences. From this perspective, underachieving students suffer a deficit of information and experiences more so than mediation. Let me segue for a moment to discuss this important difference between purposeful mediation of concepts and cognitive functions and trying to fill a kid's head with information or experience generally.

When I began to work in this field in the mid-1990s, I would speak with teachers, principals and parents about why they thought some children didn't learn as well as others. In casual conversations, many would cite a prominent research study that revealed that students from poorer socioeconomic backgrounds heard significantly fewer spoken words in their households than wealthier students. Or they would simply recount how poor kids never got to visit the Lincoln Memorial or Yellowstone like when they were a kid.

Congruent to this, conversations in the education media seemed to reflect a belief that poor achievement was mostly a function of a deficit of 'learning inputs' into the world of the student. In workshops, this perspective would rear its head when someone might ask me, "How can you ask students to think (through questions) if they haven't heard or seen enough information generally?" I would counter, "But haven't the students been in school already for several years?" The gist of most replies was that school was not a sufficient input of information/experience to make up for their low stimuli childhoods. The students didn't have enough direct learning experiences, was the belief.

Clouds and Car Accidents

I remember my mother used to lament this explanation about why some students failed to learn. She used to say that poor students experienced the world just as other children did with a continuous barrage of stimuli each moment of the day. The problem wasn't the lack of exposure to information, content or experiences reaching low socioeconomic students. It was the lack of good mediation of those same experiences that most all of us have.

I think we must have been walking outside when my mom was talking to me one day. It was a cloudy day and our faces were caught between bands of light and shadow. I thought, "The sunlight falls mostly equally upon us in spite of the shadows." That is, most poor and wealthy students receive plenty of direct exposure to information but, just like my mom said, the quality of mediation by their parents is not the same.

Returning for a moment to that prominent study, in my opinion, it is not primarily the hearing of more words that benefits the wealthy student. It's that behind the words there is the intentional mediation of a learning experience. The wealthier parent is trying to communicate meaning, while the poorer parent is just talking, is one way of describing it. Words without meaning become just so much pablum.

I am often reminded of the substantial difference between a mediated learning event and a poorly mediated event by something that happened to me in the mid-1990s. When I was in law school in Chicago, I lived in a low socioeconomic neighborhood. I saw a mother with four or five children in tow walking along a sidewalk. I soon heard the sound of a car accident. The mother turned her attention to the car accident and encouraged her kids to become excited, "Look at that! Wow!" Quickly, the children became overly excited. On a dime, the mother snapped at her children to stop looking at the accident and be quiet, "Stop looking at that! Get over here! Get back on the sidewalk.

What are you thinking?" The children looked puzzled. Frankly, so was I. I also stepped back on the sidewalk, I admit.

Years later, I was talking with a friend on her speakerphone as she was driving with her young son in a rear car seat. I heard some unusual noise, and I could tell that the phone had slipped from her hands. Knowing I would be worried, she shouted to me there had been a car accident and she couldn't reach the phone. I stayed on the phone to make sure everything was okay and got to listen to her talk to her son. She asked him several questions, "Are you okay, Graeme? I can't see the accident, where is it? Is anybody hurt? How do you know nobody is hurt? Oh, so they are leaving the car and the airbags are on? Do you think I should call the police? Oh, someone has his phone out already? Okay, Graeme, so does this show you why I can't help you play your game on your [gaming device]? And do you understand why you have to stay in the back seat?"

For me, both scenarios came to represent the stimuli that the world brings to students purposefully or inadvertently. We will each see a car accident or sit in a math class or get to read books or watch information on a screen. It's the quality of the mediation more so than the quantity of "experience" that makes the difference in the learning outcomes for the student.

Remarkably, to my knowledge, in his thinking-skills program, Dr. Feuerstein did not describe in any great detail how exactly to create the mediated learning experiences he considered so important. Surely, by structuring his curriculum without explicit instructions, he created a need system for the student and teacher to engage each other from the very start of instruction.

But the means of mediation described by Dr. Feuerstein were fairly broad and included talking or telling or what we might consider to be lecture, questioning, and certainly modeling the learning process for and with students. His point was, the learner's mind (read: cognitive acts) were at each moment the focus of instruction.

Still, Dr. Feuerstein didn't elaborate about precisely how to create MLEs with detailed instruction. Maybe Dr. Feuerstein just got tired after creating the curriculum? With his white beard, I just imagine him saying, "Eh, on this sixth day, I....forget it. You'll figure it out." I guess it was Dr. Feuerstein's rest day; he was Jewish, after all, as was my dad.

A Desert Discovery

It was my dad, Dr. Lee Hannel, who actually took Dr. Feuerstein's concept of the MLE and focused on how questions could trigger them to occur. When I asked my dad how or why he came to focus on the act of questioning as the primary means of creating mediation, he told me a story that took him to the desert communities of southern California, which at the time were rural, agricultural, poor and mostly Hispanic, and probably still are that way today.

A superintendent in a district there noted that when my dad used Dr. Feuerstein's materials, he relied mostly on asking extended series of questions to bring students to understand what they needed to do. He noticed that my dad did not allow students to decline to be questioned or say "I don't know," and he seemed to have specific strategies for making students participate. He asked my dad to describe his "pedagogy of questioning."

My dad went on to create some handouts that formed what was improvidently titled, "Cognitive Education Methodology for Teaching Content, K-12." It was and is an accurate title of our work, but really wasn't so great for marketing purposes. My dad created a handout of a few pages that listed the basic rules he followed to deal with students who did not want to participate or answer questions, i.e., behavioral deficits. He also described the sequence of questions he used to elicit understanding, i.e., cognitive functions. The list of cognitive functions or steps went deeper than parroting Bloom's Taxonomy, as it also addressed what Dr. Feuerstein called the "cognitive dysfunctions" that students might experience throughout the steps of cognition.

My dad was a big believer in not just lecturing about his questioning strategies but actually demonstrating them in front of teachers with groups of students. During workshops, he would even ask for the more challenging students from a class to form the bulk of the students in any demonstration group. I think he just wanted to prove that the strategies he formalized were truly powerful and would work with low-achieving students, not just the gifted and talented students who often were the recipients of most classroom questions. For many years, questioning was the province of "GT" programs for the gifted and talented, not the average or below-average student.

An Initiation Into Questioning

I got involved with questioning and teaching mostly by accident. I was a student at Northwest University Law School in Chicago in 1995, my final year. My dad called me at the beginning of the school year and told me that I had to help him give some workshops because his other trainers were busy--and my tuition bill had come in. With nothing more than my dad's outline of behavioral and cognitive strategies, I began to both give workshops and try out the strategies with classes of students during the live student demos. I was literally learning and teaching the strategies on the fly.

My first week of workshops was startling. What most impressed me was when I did the live student demos for teachers. I received a great deal of positive feedback from both the students themselves and observing teachers. I would hear comments like, "Can you be our teacher?" or "I never saw Jim answer that sort of question before." But I didn't feel like I was somehow predisposed to asking excellent questions. I just tried to implement my dad's approach to questioning and it seemed to work. I remember calling my dad up and saying how I was surprised that his strategies were so clearly effective. It was a sort of backhanded compliment, I guess. I miss him a lot nowadays.

I was equally if not more surprised--and remain so--by how many teachers told me that my dad's work was substantially different than what they saw in classrooms or learned in pre-service or during staff development. Indeed, some teachers would tell me that the strategies they were told were often the opposite of what my dad practiced or just felt different. It was like hearing about "opposite-world." It took me a while to accept that most American teachers are not taught an explicit pedagogy or model of how to ask questions to address behavioral problems, cognitive problems or both. I remember thinking it was inexplicable to ask teachers to "fix our kids" and then not give them the practical tools to do so. If you ask someone to build The Great Wall, you might want to give them at least a spade or something.

To this day, this whole lack of teacher-training in questioning strategies still puzzles me. There are only so many ways to describe how teachers actually teach. Lecture, questioning, modeling, experience, experiment and cooperative work all describe pedagogical approaches, but this list is obviously finite. Why isn't a standard model of questioning taught to all teachers? That is one of the few questions I continue to ask myself and have yet to answer. Maybe one day a good model of questioning will be taught to all teachers, but for you, I can only give my model of questioning, which starts on the following page. I hope you find it helpful to your teaching.

WHY ASK QUESTIONS

We begin our journey into questioning by considering why we ask questions in the first place. It seems obvious that asking questions is important for learning. But we should appreciate why questions are uniquely beneficial as a way of teaching. Consider the following four reasons I talk about in workshops.

Formative Assessment: What's Missing As Between the Learner and the Content

The first and most obvious reason to ask questions is to find out what students already know. Asking questions gets students to engage their own background knowledge, however deep or shallow. The wheels in their heads begin to spin, we might say.

Moreover, questioning tells us what we need to do next, instructionally, given their responses. Do we need to revisit the lecture? Are the students ready for an exam? Did they even read the selection in detail? This process has been described as "formative assessment" by some educators, as it helps form the instruction that is to follow.

When I explain this first rationale for asking questions in workshops, I often say that it shows us the distance or gap between where the learner is and where the content is. The learner is here, but the content is here. It shows us what the learner is "missing," so to speak.

Cognitive Leaps

The second reason is using questions to actually help students leap from one kind of thinking to another. We might think of this as creating "ah-ha" moments. The right question, asked at the right time, can lead the student to a new understanding. It's when we ask a question and the student says, "Oh, I didn't see that" or "So, we need to do X first?" It's moving the student to into the new zone of proximal development as Vygotsky would say. It's taking a step up the cognitive scaffold to a stronger, more complete, more nuanced understanding.

Engagement

The third reason is to get students engaged. It may sound obvious, but I'd guesstimate that somewhere between one-third and one-half of students are under-engaged or entirely disengaged from their own learning. Questions put a demand on the student to sit up and start talking about what's happening in his or her head. As my dad used to say, "I cannot do your thinking work for you and make you an independent learner." Lecture may unintentionally make a different implication: Stay silent and take notes.

Retaking the Learner's Perspective

The fourth reason is the least considered and perhaps the most interesting reason for taking the time to plan and ask questions to our students. Asking questions, as a modality of communication, forces us as teachers to re-take or re-visit the perspective of what I call the 'uninitiated learner'. The uninitiated learner is the student who doesn't want to learn, doesn't know how to learn, or both. To understand how questions can help us to see the world as the uninitiated learner might see it, take a moment to think about what we do when we lecture about or model something, and compare that to what we do when we use questions as a means of teaching.

When we lecture or model, what are we really doing? We are taking the world as we perceive it and creating a model of it in our head. That world-in-our-head then goes back out to the student using language or gestures or what have you. If you are lecturing about something that happened in 1861, you weren't there to see it, so you are recreating something in your mind originally brought to you by books or lectures or trips or whatever. However, we know that our first order understanding of that reality is not complete. So there are "intake" losses.

Then, too, only some fraction of what exists in our head actually makes it into the mind of the student. What the student actually takes from us as we lecture largely remains mostly invisible to us. We might pick up subtle hints of what our audience is thinking from a raised eyebrow or a look of agreement or confusion—maybe the kids have clickers to register understanding. But we can get so involved in our own thinking, our own reconstruction of reality that we don't even remember to engage the learner at all. We can get absorbed in our own thought processes needed to reconstruct that past reality.

When we ask questions, it's different. All questions after the first few are based on what a given student knows, sees, and perceives or says as we try to guide him or her to our own level of understanding. A student's response to an initial question guides our subsequent questions. Thus, we must take the world as the student understands it at each moment in time.

We can see how questioning is different from other modalities by considering a common experience like giving directions or instructions over the phone. If the person is lost in direction or in a task, you often will have to learn where they are by asking a bunch of questions, "What do you see?" or "What was the last intersection you passed?" or "What's to your right?" You have to engage the learner's world from their point of view at that moment. You can't just start talking about where you live and what's immediately around you: "Well, I'm just sitting here in this rockin' chair on the porch with my nice dog, Bella…"

In workshops, I say that this fourth reason for asking questions is different than the first reason we learned as above. Recall, the first reason is that questioning helps us know what the learner is "missing" from the content. This fourth reason lets us know what we, as their teacher, are missing in our own understanding of their point of view.

So it's less the distance as between the learner and the content, which is the first reason, as between us and the learner.

Questions can help us as teachers get back to what it was like to not know something. They force us to see things from the point of view of the new learner, once again. And that may be one of the most beneficial attributes to the act of questioning. Through our questions, we become like the student, new to the learning; the student, through his or her responses, becomes like the teacher, teaching us about his or her own mind.

WHEN TO ASK QUESTIONS

In the previous chapter, I suggest that there are several specific benefits to asking questions as a modality of instruction. The next item to consider is when to ask all these questions. When should we ask questions in the "instructional cycle" or sequence?

Before I describe our model of questioning, I'd just like to add a caveat that I'm in favor of asking questions as informally and as frequently as you'd like. The model of questioning in this book is not zero sum. You don't have to "save" your questions for this model of questioning. Ask questions as much as you wish. But the questioning process in this model is a bit more prescriptive, so here it is.

Logistics of Focused Questioning

In this model of questioning, we dedicate a specific amount of time a few times per week to asking questions in a more intensive way. We may take a 10 to 25 minute block of time out of a day, say three times per week, and use that time to drive instruction mostly through questions. So you have a dedicated "block" of time, at least a few times a week to ask questions in this way.

How long should your questioning last? Generally speaking, the younger the age of your students, the less time you spend asking questions in a row. First graders may have only enough attention to last through 5 to 10 minutes of intensive questioning. High school students may be able to effectively benefit from 25 minutes or more of questioning. It's really just a judgment call by the teacher.

This block of questioning forms what I call "meditation" on questioning. It is a time we give to ourselves as teachers to think about and practice our questioning. Although the students who actually participate in those three (or however many) specific segments of questioning will benefit from the participation, the "mental profits" of that time initially accrue mostly to the teacher. That is because we are dedicating a certain amount time each week to practice the art and skill of planning and asking questions for ourselves.

In workshops, I analogize that it's like setting aside time each week to practice how to shoot a free throw in basketball or how to serve a ball in tennis. You, the teacher, need to schedule a time to practice and can't just wait for those moments to come along in the game where you are at the foul line or serving the ball. Sometimes, you want to practice a narrow skill so that it becomes much more fluid when you have to use it without much preparation. Although the benefits of practice accrue to you, eventually they benefit everyone you play with, too. You getting better makes everyone better.

Planning the Imagined Conversation

It is important to note that planning the questions you intend to ask may take just as much time as asking them. Writing out the questions is the most helpful act. There seems to be something about the actual writing or typing out of questions that makes us consider what we intend to ask more thoroughly.

Generally speaking, the teacher who writes out about 15 or more questions will have enough questions to scaffold the inquiries properly for a 10-20 minute block of questioning. This is because, when you write out a question, your mind often goes forward and imagines the forthcoming chain of responses and additional questions you might need to ask. You think, "I'll ask this, but they'll say that. And then I'll ask this, but then they'll get only part of that. So I'll have to ask..." Writing out your questions leads to what I describe as better "imagined conversations." Your subconscious mind is always predicting the future, just as your body predicts that you will feel supported by the chair underneath you now and would immediately notice it if something felt amiss. This act of prediction also occurs with questions.

Eventually, the planning time will substantially diminish but should never disappear entirely. We must premeditate upon the questions we intend to ask before we ask them. Although I try to keep my legal stories to a minimum, I will share that when I take the time to write out the questions I intend to ask to a witness or expert or client, I generally do a much better job of it.

After Direct Instruction

Another key point to the timing of our instructional segment dedicated to asking questions is that it should be after direct instruction. It comes after students have a basic working knowledge of the underlying content, concept or skills required to answer your questions. In practical terms, this means students must have read the content or listened to the lecture or watched something before they are asked many questions about it.

When information becomes complex, it's hard to ask effective questions if students don't have some pre-existing knowledge about the underlying content. For instance, if students don't know any algebra and you introduce the topic with a question like, "What is a variable" or "How do we solve for one unknown?" you might get only a strange look. If you are introducing the concept of gravity to students, it'd be hard for them to answer a question like, "Why don't we fall into the sun given its larger mass?" Our model of questioning assumes students have some background knowledge so that they can meaningfully benefit from the questions we want to ask.

Please note that I am not against asking some questions even before direct instruction, though I do think we must be aware of the drawback seen above. But if those questions work for you and your students, use them.

All this approach says is that questioning works better after direct instruction and to practice the planning and asking of questions for 10-25 minutes a several times per week, if possible.

BEHAVIOR

We need to create a behavioral framework for asking questions. All forms of instruction, from lecture—"be quiet and take notes"—to questioning to cooperative learning have their own behavioral models. The short but intense periods of questioning suggested by this model—for instance, 10-25 minutes of questioning—require the teacher to ask questions and for students to think, respond, answer, ask questions to the teacher or other students, and so on. There's a lot going on.

One obvious issue with this kind of questioning is that many students don't want to participate in class. There are particular students, or even a whole class, whose behavior makes it clear they don't want to be asked questions. In some cases, it's not that students are actively disobedient or disrespectful. They may only be passive. Those passive classrooms are often the most frustrating. The potential may be there, but the desire is low. It's like all the wood is there, but no one wants to start a fire.

Overcoming attitudes that limit the student's own self-engagement is critical to using questions effectively. Methodologies that are based on questioning, but that fail to address the behavioral realities or obstacles of the classroom exist in an artificial classroom. In short, let's talk about the students who don't want to participate or need some encouragement to do so.

The Culture of Disengagement

I have given a label to those attitudes and behaviors that work against participation and questioning. I call this the "culture of disengagement." Sadly, in some places, this culture can become so embedded that teachers themselves may begin to subconsciously accept that students have a "right to be passive." The norm then becomes resisting questions or doing as little as possible to answer them. Discussions prompted by questions are extremely difficult to initiate or keep going.

In workshops, I ask my audience some questions to identify signs of a culture of disengagement, which you may consider here for yourself:

- Do some students try to avoid being asked questions?

- Would it be possible for a student to go several classes or longer without being asked an academic question?

- Do students often say, "I don't know?"

- Do you observe any "leave me alone" behaviors?

- Do students try to avoid standing out?

- Do students perceive learning as driven by internal motivations (goals) or external ones (carrots/stick)?

- Do students tell you about the things they want to learn next?

Another good question we should ask ourselves is whether our students are amazed or inspired, or at least puzzled or curious, at least once a day (if not more). Could a student go all day without wondering anything? I think, unfortunately, a lot could...

Moreover, when our questions are met with dull stares, "I don't know" or one-word responses, it's hard to feel enthusiastic for asking more questions. Worse, other borderline students can feel the negative vibe and may decide to mimic the passive student's behavior. The student who actually intends to answer with reasoning ends up looking or feeling out of place. This culture of disengagement must be challenged unless we are willing to allow students to attend school purely in body, not brain.

Some teachers resist demanding participation from students because they don't want to be viewed as coercive. They want to be friends with their students and not force anyone to participate. I agree we should try to be as friendly as possible. But my argument for asking, pushing and demanding participation goes beyond the fact that school is a fundamentally coercive act—you have to come to school and, if you are there, you might as well learn something.

The reality is, as my dad used to say many times in workshops, and I used to harass him about it but now know better, "I cannot do your thinking-work for you and make you an independent learner." When we let students opt-of of questioning too often, it's like we're letting them not do a mental pushup or sit up. If we do that too often, when they fail to achieve (mental) fitness, it shouldn't be a huge surprise.

Consider, too, that children from other countries who struggle to attend school will never understand or be empathetic to American students who had all the luxuries of going to school and didn't take advantage of it (or even worked to deny themselves of it). I've spoken with children in Mexico who spent their schooldays picking garbage out of mounds of trash or selling tortillas door to door—elementary age kids.

One time, while visiting my mother who lives in Queretaro, Mexico, I asked a young boy, maybe about ten years old, whether he would even want to go to school instead of selling tortillas all day long. The way he spoke about his dream of attending school, simply the chance to do something different and leave his environment, was profoundly sad. He knew school was critical for him, personally. He also knew he would likely never go to school.

So it's hard for me to feel badly about asking questions to American students when, for some children, the actual alternative is literally sifting through refuse or selling gum in the middle of busy street. I wonder if we, as American educators, may have gone too far in looking for our students to like us in some weird codependent relationship.

Our students must try to answer our questions. And we must try to ask them. It's as simple as that.

7 Principles and 7 Practices

How can we practically address attitudes of disengagement in students? My dad created a set of seven "principles," each of which has a corresponding "practice," to address the most common symptoms of disengagement. Each principle is really a belief that contributes to a culture of engagement, while each practice is the implementation of that belief in a practical way—the "action." The principles lead to the practices; our beliefs lead to our actions.

Giving some attention and thought to the principles before considering the practices is very important. Don't just "jump" to the practice in your mind. In workshops, I purposely show participants a principle and have them discuss it before eventually revealing the specific practice associated with it. In my experience, the teacher who does not contemplate his or her beliefs—which are embedded in the principles— is less likely to stick with the practices.

Consider for a moment how beliefs lead to practices. Maybe a student will pay lip service to the importance of studying. But if you spend enough time asking them about it, maybe their real belief is that they just want a passing score and that's enough to keep them out of trouble—off the school's or their parents' radar. Their belief leads to the action (or inaction) of not studying too much. This example may show why "beliefs" are so important. They are like concepts in that respect. They provide a superstructure or architecture for our thinking or lack thereof.

In workshops, I like to share a Chinese proverb from a general named Sun Tsu, who is famous for his pithy sayings about strategy, conflict, and so on. In one saying, Sun Tsu said, "Strategy without tactics is the slowest route to victory. Tactics without strategy is the noise before defeat."

What Sun Tsu says could be related to effective questioning. Admittedly, I've modified it's wording to suit my purpose here. But to me, what Sun Tsu says it that having tactics (or "practices/actions") for questioning—ask this, ask that—isn't enough. We must have a belief system, which Sun Tsu labels as a strategy, to put those practices into a framework. So, the time spent thinking about the strategies or what I call principles is just as important as the time spent memorizing the specific practices. We can't just know "what" to do, we must have a "why" behind doing it.

Speaking of the behavioral practices, you will quickly notice that the practices are mostly behavioral in character and relatively explicit or concrete or practical. They are the "doing," if you prefer. If a student does X, you do Y. Understanding the practices isn't usually a problem. The difficulty is that even though the practices are simple to understand, they may be hard to actually enact. I think they become hard to enact because we may unconsciously hold conflicting beliefs or principles about students, learning, autonomy, school and the nature of participation.

In sum, we must consider or reflect upon our true principles before we look to our practices; our beliefs guide our actions. To counter a culture of disengagement, we must have firm beliefs about the potential of our students to participate in their own learning before we will likely do what is required to overcome any disengagement.

Let's begin with our first principle (belief) and practice (action).

PRINCIPLE ONE

We believe that students come to school with the need to learn, and when they are in school, they do not have the right not to learn.

Our first principle is a belief that some students come to school with a need to learn that they may not recognize or self-perceive. They show up to the classroom, but when we ask questions, they don't want to answer. They are there, but in a way, they are not. Their reasons for avoiding participation may include fear of embarrassment to simply being tired or uninterested in the subject matter.

We may even empathize with the student who does not feel like participating by answering our questions. At times, we may have felt the same way when we were students. But we still must ask that non-participating or disinterested student some questions. This is a key, albeit simple idea.

School is a requirement, not an option. If school were entirely voluntary, perhaps we could accept students who would elect not to learn. We could just move on to another student. But at this moment in time, school is mandatory, and this means that learning itself is actually mandatory. Learning is not optional or discretionary or even really a choice.

More practically, if you do not participate, I cannot really tell whether you are learning or how much you are learning. I can't see inside your head without your own voice, at least at this point in the technological scheme of things. There is no technology that allows me to know what you are presently thinking. So I must ask you questions to know what is in your head and fulfill the purpose of school.

Practice 1: Involuntary Questioning

Given the first belief, what should be our first practice? It could be described as "involuntary questioning," which is what my dad called it. This means we ask questions to any and all students without hesitation. If the student has his hand up, I may ask him a question. But if a student has her hand down, I may still ask her a question. Smiling or frowning, I ask questions.

As my dad would say in workshops, he liked to imagine all his students waving both hands, dying to participate. It was a mental image that allowed him to call on students whose demeanor could sometimes be described as, "Don't bother me" or worse. My dad was a very, very kind man, so he really didn't want to make a student feel badly. But he knew he had to still involve them in the questioning or try to. Again, that's why he would say, "I cannot do your thinking-work for you and make you an independent learner."

As with any practice, we have to be reasonable. Perhaps a student just walked in the room and is getting settled--probably not the right moment to ask a question. If the student seems very upset for some reason, again, not a good time to throw a series of questions to him or her. Our questions aren't designed to embarrass or catch a student off-guard. There should be no interest in a "Gotcha!" opportunity. That's not our motivation. You'd be surprised how often questions are used more to correct behavior than to enhance cognition.

One well-known education commentator has cleverly disparaged this kind of questioning of students as a form of "cold calling" like telemarketers do. But unlike a telemarketer, we're not calling on the students to sell them a product to secure money for ourselves, we're calling on them to get them to use their minds to benefit them. I can't do your thinking work for you, and I can't know what you are thinking until you tell me. So, you have to participate at least a bit. While involuntary questioning can be done poorly, so, too, can all other kinds of instruction.

In sum, our proposition to our students is a fairly reasonable one. For the short time we dedicate to this kind of questioning, maybe only 10-25 minutes once a day, I have the right to call on you because you came to school with a need to learn, and whether or not you understand that right now, I do. Thus, I will ask you a least a few questions to get to you truly be present in this moment of learning.

Norms in Conflict—Autonomy v. Participation

Given how clear-cut this practice is, why are so few classrooms run according to this basic understanding, one that most teachers and many parents would, if they thought about it, probably affirm? Why are there so many non-participatory students? I think we might be seeing two different cultural norms (aka, principles) in conflict, and if we understand this tension, we can make a better decision about what we require in terms of classroom participation.

One norm we value is giving people space or the right to privacy generally. For instance, imagine I am in an elevator and you walk in, but rather than greet you, I stare at my phone, newspaper or feet. I'm giving you a clear message without me actually saying anything to you: Leave me alone. And generally speaking, most people, including teachers, naturally disengage when they don't see any form of reciprocal behavior.

A second norm is the norm of participation required by school. Back in the elevator under this norm, you might still press me by saying, "Hello. Welcome to the academic elevator! I have a question to ask you about what you are reading." Yes, that would be a unique experience! The point is that as teachers, this second norm—the norm of engagement—is perhaps the key function of school and overrules the right to personal autonomy most of the time.

It is important for us to reconcile ourselves to the fact that by its very nature, questioning is different than other modes of instruction because it is more imposing. It demands the other's—the learner's— attention. When we acknowledge this, we don't feel so bad about those weighted seconds that go by after you've asked a question and the student glares at you, looks for peer reinforcement, and then grudgingly gives you back a response. Hopefully, this only describes the rare hard-knocks sort of student.

Remember, the actual questioning may only last for a minute or so with any given student, at most, and the whole process lasts between 10 to 25 minutes, usually, so it's not like this is some endurance race of terrible, mean questions. It's just saying, "Hey, get involved here for a small fraction of the day and let me hear your voice to know what's in your brain." It's very hard to know what a student is actually thinking if they remain totally quiet.

Our first strategy requires our rational persistence in asking questions to reluctant students.

Practice: Involuntary questioning of all students.

PRINCIPLE TWO

We believe that students are temporarily under-trained, not permanently under-brained; they are dormant, not dead.

Our second principle requires us to assume that most of our students can answer the questions we want to ask. It's a sort of belief in the "brain" of the student. It's a confidence that most students can answer the question we want to ask at that moment. So, if I want to ask a particular question, I will not reserve it primarily for the students who are likely to answer it successfully. I ask it to any student in the room, randomly if I so chose.

Let's imagine you have a class that has the full range of students from overachieving to under-performing, a normal inclusion setting. Our vision of the class and our internal metrics may tell us that only some students are capable of answering a question that we want to ask at a given moment. So we may want to give each student the "right" question for them at that moment. We want students to feel successful or reinforced. So we tend to give students questions that are geared towards a successful outcome.

But there is a trade-off. If we attempt to tailor our questions to each student all the time, we may end up having different conversations at different levels with different groups of students. Some students get "good" or higher order questions or simply more questions, while others get the "Who is buried in Grant's tomb?" type of questions or only the occasional question.

The problem with having several kinds of conversations at once is more than logistical, though it is pretty hard to ask "A" level questions to the A students, "B" level questions to the B students, "C" level questions to the C students, and so on, and continue to develop the same thread of conversation for everyone in the room.

The more fundamental problem if we attempt to tailor too much is this: If we fail to ask the C student the A level question and they rarely get exposed to it, how can we ever expect them to answer that kind of question? Intuitively, we may wish to ask the C student a C level question or C+ question so that they will be successful right then—and there is a strong role for that approach, too--but sometimes we need to ask the sort of question that's far ahead of where that particular student may actually be mentally. We have to ask them the question that is a big stretch so that at the very least, they will have been exposed to what the standard is for everyone.

In this respect, we are going farther than the zone of proximal development at least once in a while. In this way, we purposefully may invite "failure" rather than success, but that is okay. Obviously, we hope the student makes the big leap, but if she doesn't, that doesn't imply that the question wasn't proper. Sometimes, we ask a question just to let students know what we're going for. And it helps to teach the student the idea of resilience, and that being "wrong" is okay--the path to success or understanding isn't just about getting all the correct answers right off the bat.

Practice 2: Equalizing the Quantity and Quality of Questions

Our second principle is implemented in two ways. The first practice considers the quantity of questions each student receives over a period of time. The second practice considers the quality of those same questions.

In terms of quantity, if we believe in the equal potential of students, we hope to ask about the same number of questions to all students over time. If Maria is asked twenty questions in a two-week period but John is only asked three questions, we can see that Maria has been given more thinking-opportunities.

It is important to stress that being equal in terms of quantity is measured over time, not in a single instructional segment lasting 15 minutes. In a single class period, one student may need more questions than another to come to an understanding or cross a thinking-threshold. But over time, we hope to provide equal opportunities to think via our questions to all students.

Please note that it is not whether a student can successfully answer all the questions we ask that is the point here, only that we have asked the questions and thus given them opportunities to think. In this regard, we mostly measure ourselves, here. Are we being equal in the quantity of question-opportunities? You may keep a checklist of how many questions you've asked each student to ensure you are spreading the wealth equally. Just put a check mark down next to the student's name each time you ask them a question, then re-check your list at the end of the week. Notice if you some students are inadvertently being missed or skipped over.

Quality of Questions

The second way of implementing our second principal involves the quality of questions. In terms of quality, we should feel free to ask the A level question (or B level or whatever) to the C or D or B student, acknowledging in advance that those students will probably not answer the question as well as the A student at first. If it is time to ask, "What's the main idea of the chapter?" we feel at liberty to ask that to any student and not just the ones who seem perfectly ready for it.

What should we do when the A level question--or just the question we want to ask--doesn't work? Well, try asking the B level question and then the C level question. Scaffold down the questioning ladder in terms of the cognitive difficulty of the question. Or change the language of the question. Or break the question up into addressing smaller pieces of content, for instance, a question about the page becomes a question about a paragraph.

The student we call upon may not be able to answer our initial question, but at least they can say they have heard that kind of question, that they've had a chance to think. Move on if the student is unable to answer after trying out a few more questions that are lower on the scaffold.

Once, during a live student demo, I asked a student a question and he wasn't able to answer it and struggled as well with a few of my follow-up questions. A teacher in the workshop asked me why I thought the student couldn't answer my questions. I turned it around and asked the teacher for her intuition. She said, "Maybe he has never been asked those kinds of questions before?" Perhaps, I replied, "And whose fault would that be?"

A Culture of Effort

An introspective question we might ask ourselves is why, as teachers, are we sometimes afraid to ask the harder questions to certain students. A reasonable explanation is that we want to scaffold our questions; we don't want a question to be too far a mental leap.

Another explanation is, "I don't want to embarrass the student." We may remember a time when we were asked a question, didn't know how to respond, and were left feeling stupid—the dreadful pause of, "Uhhh."

But I think there is something else going on that is unaccounted for. As teachers, I think we may subconsciously feel that if a student cannot answer our questions, then we have failed them. The hearing of an inadequate response by a student makes us feel bad, too. We want to hear correct, convergent responses not just to keep the students feeling good but to keep ourselves feeling good. Some people might describe this as a form of co-dependence.

We should ask ourselves as educators why this co-dependence has come about? Why is it that our esteem and our students' esteem has become so tied up with being able to answer a particular question or two in any one moment? Why can't we accept the reality that perhaps only some of our questions will work, and it's nobody's fault when a question isn't immediately answered well.

I describe this situation as an artifact of the 'culture of success' that is part of our education culture. As educators, we are often talking and thinking about student success. How many posters in hallways talk about "SUCCESS." I don't disparage the goal. But in terms of questioning, if we become so concerned with hearing immediate success and reinforcing short-term success, we may forget that what usually determines success in the long haul is effort.

Effective questioning demands a culture of effort, not reinforcement of every minor success. The student should say to herself: "I may not know the answer right now, but I will try very hard to think about what it might be. I know that my effort is the key ingredient."

What this means concretely is that we don't expect all of our questions to work immediately, and we don't hesitate to ask the harder questions to students who aren't immediately ready for them. We want give them a sense of what the standard is, where we are going.

If I ask one hundred questions, perhaps only sixty of them will be correctly answered. The others may be off the mark, incorrect or divergent but I don't give up. I don't say, "No, that's wrong, let's stop here." I simply ask another question, maybe phrased differently or lower on the cognitive scaffold.

The visitor to my room might object, "Wait, that student, even after three questions, didn't get the right answer. Won't he feel badly?" To which I would reply, what makes you think that his self-esteem is, or should be, dependent on answering a few questions on a Tuesday afternoon? It may be the case that we have imposed our own fears and insecurities on the students—know this right now, please, won't you? Our practice should instead be to ask the questions we want and see what happens. If it's time to ask a question, it's time to ask it to most any student in the room.

A good way of thinking about this is to select the question you want to ask and then ask it to any student. Choose the question, then the student. Oppositely, if we think of a specific student, first, we are likely to tailor our questions only to their current level of thinking. So don't think, "I wonder what I can ask John/Pedro/Jessica?" Instead, think,

"What do I want to ask? Okay, I'll ask that to anyone I want, as I believe you all want to answer!"

Practice: Try to equalize the quantity and quality of questions; select the question, then the student.

PRINCIPLE THREE

We believe in getting students to do
most of the thinking-work.

Our third principle proposes that the primary purpose of asking questions is to shift the burden of thinking to our students and to encourage participation generally. Asking lots of questions helps us to achieve both goals. It's a bit of an oversimplification, but asking fifty questions is generally better than asking five questions is a way of putting it. Each question is yet another demand for the students to think. Still, be careful not to mistake quantity for quality. Sometimes, fewer questions, more thoughtfully posed, create better thinking-opportunities than too many bite-sized questions.

Still, the more questions you ask, the more likely every student in the room will be given an opportunity to think. But keep a pace that you and the students feel comfortable with.

Asking more questions also makes the cognitive leaps we ask students to take easier to bridge. Imagine trying to climb a ladder to the third story of a building. If the ladder has forty rungs, it's probably a lot easier to climb than a ladder with just ten footholds. More questions usually means an easier cognitive ascent.

One benefit to asking more questions is that it tends to make students feel more willing to participate in the first place. Many students fear being asked questions because they feel their success is contingent on "answering right." The fewer the questions asked, the more weight is placed on each query. When there is an abundance of questions in the room, students will inevitably hear both convergent and divergent answers from other students. They'll hear both "good" and "bad" answers. From this, students come to learn that participation is just as important as "being right" with a particular answer and that no single question or answer is that pivotal for goodness' sake.

Finally, an environment of lots of questions makes students more willing to ask questions to us. How many times did we, as students, want to ask a question but didn't do so because no one else did before us? As teachers, we must do more than just say, "Does anyone have any questions about this?" We must model that behavior and actually ask a lot of questions to get things started. The teacher's asking of lots of questions ultimately translates into a security blanket for students to ask some questions back to us or to each other.

Stay in Questioning Mode

So, during the time allocated to questioning, we try to stay in questioning or asking mode. A big challenge with staying in asking mode is that when students don't give us the answers we want to hear, some of us will automatically revert to telling. That is, we revert to lecture, showing, explaining, hinting or helping and sometimes, even answering our own questions! If we have decided to ask questions for 20 minutes, but then spend 10 minutes going back over things by lecturing and showing, we've obviously reduced our time for questioning in half.

Be careful not to answer your own questions. When we do that, it's like we are saying, "Let me ask my best student this question. Oh, that would be me. Well done!" The more we, as teachers, do of the telling, hinting, helping and showing, the more we shift the thinking-work back to ourselves and decrease participation. If I, as the teacher, do the moving, lifting, carrying—the physical work—how is that different from doing all the mental work by answering our own questions?

Some students have even learned to feign ignorance--"I don't know"--to get us to move back to telling and showing and helping generally. It's often easier for them to be shown than to show us. But that defeats the purpose of our questions. Let's keep our students doing most of the thinking.

Though we ask a lot of questions, we must remember to listen to answers and give wait-time when needed. There is no point in asking a lot of questions if we can't wait and listen to the responses to them. If a student becomes shaky when answering, we can always give him or her a little help with another question to nudge his or her thinking along.

Practice: Try to stay in asking mode and refrain from telling, showing, hinting or answering your own questions.

PRINCIPLE FOUR

We inquire to hear reasoning, not answers.

Our fourth principle says that we value a student's response mostly for the reasoning behind it. Some students have learned to give cursory initial responses hoping the teacher will go away thereafter. Then, when asked a follow-up question about why they think something, they may reply with "because" or "because it says so."

My mom used to characterize these kinds of usually one-word responses as egocentric. The students must assume that their thinking is obvious to others and doesn't require elaboration. I'm always reminded of the book *The Hitchhiker's Guide to the Galaxy* when students give these one-word or very brief answers. In that book, the answer to the "question of the universe" is simply the number 42. Students who give answers without reasoning make me think of someone just telling me, "42." What does that mean?

We want to structure our questions so that our students learn to embed their reasoning into their initial response. We want students to move away from one-word answers. Students must go beyond saying, "I think it is X." Better would be, "I think it is X because of Y and Z." They must learn to see that every response must include a reason or supporting evidence. Show me where your thinking is coming from, please.

Question-Response-Question

To get students to include reasoning with every response, our fourth practice is to follow a pattern called Question-Response-

Question or QRQ. We ask a question, elicit a response, and follow up with another question or two to learn the reasoning behind the initial response or extend that reasoning.

Usually, the student who provides the initial response is asked to give the reasoning for it. But we can ask a question to John, hear his response, and then ask Mary to support, extend, or critique John's answer. This makes sure that students are paying attention to other students and a varied approach helps. It also gives students a chance to understand another student's thinking by trying to support or amend it.

Many times, the follow up question is just "why." Why do you think that? But you can put it in other ways. Where is that in the text? What supports your thinking? How can you prove that? Even saying, "Tell me more about that" will sometimes help develop their reasoning. For younger students, you might follow up with, "Okay, but how would you explain that to your younger brother or sister? Like, why does that make sense?"

Show your own curiosity about their thinking. My dad used to say you have to learn how to play "dumb" in a really smart way to get some student to give more than just the first thing that comes to their head.

Don't forget to enact the QRQ process both with correct and incorrect, convergent and divergent answers, whether oral or written. Imagine there is a formal, correct answer to a question on a multiple-choice exam, answer "C." Maria selects a poor answer, A. Without changing your expression to reflect any disappointment, ask, "Maria, how did you get A?" or "Why is A correct?" If the next student, James, gives the correct answer C, still ask, "How did you get C, James?"

You may also ask the students to enact the QRQ process among and between each other. One common tactic is to ask students to agree or disagree with another student's response. This can be effective as both a tool for justification and also for learning how to critique an answer in a respectful way.

One drawback with this technique above is that sometimes students overly personify the process or end up feeling personally criticized. It may be necessary to teach students to reframe this process from saying, "I disagree with John's answer because" to, "I disagree with that understanding because…"

Again, my preferred way of effectuating the QRQ process is simply to ask the student, "And what is your reasoning?" or "Where is that in the text?" or simply "Can you justify that for me?" But there are many ways to crack a nut, I suppose, so do what seems most effective towards achieving justification of the initial response.

Affirming Right Answers and Correcting Wrong Ones

One query that comes up in workshops when discussing justification of a response is when to affirm or oppositely correct a student's response? Do we say "good job!" or "great answer" after the student has given an initial response, if correct, or do we wait until they have justified their response? In this approach, we must learn to affirm the effort to justify rather than the initial response given. We're not affirming the actual answer so much as the efforts made towards finding it.

Consider the following situation involving Juan and Bill. Bill answers a question and the teacher says, "That's right. How'd you get that?" Bill gives his explanation, which is sufficient. Then, the teacher asks Juan a question and he responds but not quite as well. The teacher then says, "Okay, how'd you get that?" It seems just the smallest change in intonation between hearing "That's right" and "Okay," but Juan probably now thinks he has selected an incorrect answer because he didn't hear the "That's right." He probably won't want to explain himself at this point, because he may believe that is wrong. Indeed, some students immediately think that an answer must be wrong because we've asked them to justify it!

So, in this approach, it is only after both Juan and Bill respond with reasoning that we say "good job" to either of them. Even when a response is actually incorrect we can affirm the effort towards reasoning, if the effort is in fact good, "I can see why you thought that" or "That reasoning is very good even if it wasn't the correct answer." Oppositely, a correct or convergent response without reasoning isn't worth very much in the long term.

If a student's response is not correct, we still ask them to justify it. We do the exact same thing as if their response were correct. Sometimes, upon closer examination, the student will change his answer. Or by their attempt at justification, we will come to understand exactly where their misunderstanding comes from. So we must allow and in fact require the student to justify both the "right" and "wrong" answer. We can take corrective action through additional questions after the student has been asked to justify a bit more.

A final note is to ask students to support their thinking using resources like the textbook. This helps them on more than just tests. Other students may not know exactly where a student has found her reasoning if the teacher only says, "That's right." The more the student who is responding is asked to show exactly where his or her thinking comes from, the better it is for other students. Besides, there are simply too many textbooks and resources that just sit there and aren't used as supporting evidence for thinking.

Practice: Follow a QRQ pattern in your questions whenever possible. Initial (Q)uestion—student's initial (R)esponse—follow-up (Q)uestion for justification.

PRINCIPLE FIVE

*We believe in maintaining a positive
environment of inquiry.*

Our fifth principle notes that one of the drawbacks of questioning is getting frustrated when students aren't answering in the ways we'd like. When that happens, we may end up asking questions that are negative in tone or inquiry. Negative questions decrease student participation dramatically. Who would want to participate in a negative environment?

Recognizing what makes a question negative may helps us to avoid asking such questions. There are two ways by which questions may be interpreted negatively. Questions can be negative in tone. We may reasonably ask, "Why do you think that?" or turn negative with "Why do you think THAT?" Prefacing a question with a negative comment can make the whole question negative, for instance, "I know you probably won't be able to answer this, but what...?"

Other kinds of questions are negative regardless of their tone. They are negative because of their inquiry; what they ask is not appropriate. Rhetorical questions tend to be negative. One example of such a question is, "Is that really a fifth grade kind of answer?" It denigrates the student's response and doesn't ask for anything to boot. We might as well say, "Do you have an undiagnosed cognitive problem that no one knows about?"

Stay Neutral and Say "Thank You"

We should endeavor to keep our questions neutral in tone and inquiry. We try not to allow ourselves to appear frustrated with the questions we ask. Our questions aren't rhetorical.

If we find that our questions are leading to frustration, we have the option of ending the questioning process. Maybe, after a few questions, we realize that our students needed a stronger lecture prior to questioning, or we feel that the questioning is now beginning to go off-task. What to do? Simply thank the students and end the process like this: "Okay, we're shifting gears now. Thank you for answering my questions. Let's move on to something else."

For whatever reason, saying "thank you" seems to be a graceful exit to interaction. Consider how when we go to a store, often the clerk will say "thank you" and Americans will usually respond with "thank you." We probably aren't truly thanking them for charging us, but acknowledging that our interaction has come to an end.

Saying "thank you" works just as well when considering the individual student who is having trouble responding. Let's say John is stuck trying to respond and the seconds seem to pass like minutes. Other students may want to answer or help John. Try not to say, "John, I'll get back to you later," just say, "Thank you" and move on to another student. I've found that saying, "I'll come back to you later" can make the student feel badly, sort of acknowledging his or her failure. Oppositely, for whatever reason, saying "thank you" does not connote a particular judgment, just, "I have to go now."

You can certainly get back to John if you have the time and it seems right to do so. By thanking John, you don't leave him feeling like he failed. You recognize his effort but simply need to move on and so the "thank you" is a nice, easy way of breaking the questioning process with a student who is stuck on something. This applies equally well for the student who won't keep his hand down and wants to monopolize the engagement.

The basic concept here is simple. Negativity decreases participation. Good questions can become negative questions, so be aware of this. If your questions aren't going where you want, you always have the option of ending the questioning process by simply saying, "Thank you."

Practice: Keep your questions neutral or positive in tone and end the process with a "thank you" if necessary.

PRINCIPLE SIX

*We want to discourage
episodic learning.*

Our sixth principle recognizes that for some students, questions are almost like an invitation to guess. Maybe the student doesn't want to invest effort into thinking at that moment. Guessing is an easy way out.

Underachieving students perceive that guessing has some chance at solving their immediate problem, which may be as basic as hoping the teacher will simply move on if their guess is correct or seems convergent enough. It's the gambler's approach to learning. As I sometimes say in workshops, underachieving students like to guess like gamblers like to gamble. We want to discourage this episodic or random approach to answering questions.

No Guessing

Our sixth practice is that we avoid asking students questions that solicit them to guess, such as, "Can anybody take a guess?" Better to encourage students not to guess, "No guesses, please."

The tone of our questions may encourage guessing. It's one thing to ask, "What do you think?" and another to ask, "What do you thiiiiiiink?" The former is more neutral and requests thinking; the latter seems to solicit any kind of response at all. I always think of the movie Ferris Bueller's Day Off where the teacher is almost begging for participation, "Bueller? Anyone? Bueller? Anyone?"

We may inadvertently encourage guessing by suggesting the answer we want to hear through our questions. A good example of this would be when we ask, "Could it be D?" Students usually will agree with us and select the answer we suggest through the question, in this case "D." We can avoid this situation by asking, "What could it be?" rather than "Could it be D?"

Please note that though we don't want students to guess, we aren't saying they should not be asked to predict or to estimate. If you'd like a student to predict something, ask them to predict. If you want them to estimate, ask them to estimate. The issue is that for students with a tendency towards episodic learning behaviors, guessing promotes mostly a random approach to answering questions and reduces their incentive to think even a little bit before they speak.

Practice: Don't ask students to guess and discourage guess-making behavior.

PRINCIPLE SEVEN

We believe that 'I don't know' is a learned behavior often used to avoid engagement.

Our seventh principle assumes that most students often know more than they are willing to share. One of the most common behaviors used to avoid participation is when students reply with "I don't know." Some students simply state the words; others just shrug or stare blankly. I've heard of students writing and even speaking out loud, "I.D.K."

This sort of behavior often convinces us to move along in our questions. The cultural norm is for the teacher to ask a question, get an "I don't know" and frequently just move on to another student. When students observe a teacher move on immediately after an "I don't know" response, a mimicking behavior may occur. The next student's response also becomes "I don't know." If we don't find a way to overcome this behavior, it really doesn't matter how beneficial our questions may be. We've got to discourage the I.D.K.

1-3 More Questions After An "I.D.K."

Our strategy to reduce hearing "I don't know" is simple and behavioral. When we hear those words, rather than immediately moving on to another student, we try to think of at least one more question to ask the student who says it, if not two or three more questions.

Note that we usually do not ask more than an additional one, two or three questions after hearing "I don't know"; more questions than that may make the tone of things confrontational as opposed to simply curious. Other students may also tune out if they feel one student is going to carry the load of questions for an extended period of time. So, if you don't get anything after a few more questions, you may have to move on. Don't feel bad about that.

I can't say exactly what the few extra questions subsequent to the "I don't know" should be. You might decide to work your way back through some of the previous questions. We just want students to internalize that the easiest way to be left alone is to try to respond rather than reflexively blurt out, "I don't know." And don't forget that even when the student gives a response, he must still be asked to justify, elaborate or explain what supports it.

One tactic that seems to work when students say "I don't know" is to quickly ask a few questions that you are sure the student is able to answer. You sort of rebuild the momentum of the student and then present him or her with the question that elicited the "I don't know" in the first place. Sometimes, just by reiterating what the student does know, they are able to give a response better than "I don't know."

Teachers have also told me they have found success by doing a "thumbs up/down" where they will ask the student those re-scaffolding questions but ask the student to signal their understanding with a thumb up or thumb down, and in that way get the student to start thinking again rather than just be satisfied with "I don't know."

I have also found that sometimes, you can pretend you didn't even hear the "I don't know" response and just ask the question one more time and the student may actually answer. But you have to really pretend that you don't "get" what the student is saying by "I don't know." It might go sort of like this:

Teacher: So, what can you infer from the second line of the problem?

Student: I don't know.

Teacher: Right. Okay. So, what can you infer from the second line of the problem?

In the situation above, the failure to acknowledge the initial response of "I don't know" may trigger the student to think something like, "Huh, I just said I don't know and she still is asking me the same question. She must be really dense! I'll have to actually answer this because she just has no idea what I'm saying here." Of course, this is all a big gambit that the student really does have a sense of the answer, and it depends on how well you can play "dumb" as a teacher. But I've seen and heard it work, so throw it in your arsenal of questioning-tricks.

Another tactic that I have been told works is to acknowledge the student who said I don't know and then say, "Okay, here's another question for you. You just don't know right now."

A tactic that does not seem to work particularly well is to ask the student, "Well, what DO you know?" Depending on how you frame that question, this may create some friction between you and the student(s). But if this has worked for you, use it accordingly.

I acknowledge that pressuring a student with more questions after an "I don't know" may cause some tension. Younger students may give an "I don't know" because they really don't know. Still, asking more questions will help them come to know. We cut older students less slack, obviously.

When struggling with "I don't know" behaviors, it helps to acknowledge that our American culture doesn't like it when people give up on trying to know. Imagine you ask your doctor for her diagnosis and she simply shrugs, or your car mechanic or the bank that deposited your check. By fighting against "I don't know," we introduce students to the values of our culture and hopefully help them approach the world with an attitude that says, "I may not know right now, but I'm going to try to find out!"

Practice: Immediately ask one, two, or three more questions to the student who has just said, "I don't know."

COGNITIVE FRAMEWORK

A strong behavioral framework to challenge disengagement is critical to getting all students to participate. But the primary purpose of questioning is not just participation. We want to engender with students a process of critical thinking. By critical thinking, I mean the direct application of cognitive skills to specific sets of information.

Sadly, in education, there really has not been much attention given to an overarching framework for developing thinking by asking questions. Often, teachers have not gotten any training in how to ask questions beyond being provided with lists of question-stems and a mandatory mention of Bloom's Taxonomy. While I think the intent is good, I don't think you can make questioning mechanical. The teacher needs to have an internal process for forming his or her questions, and a deep understanding as to why that process is likely to be effective. It seems crazy to me, the idea that you can get critical thinking out of students, through questions which were themselves created without the input of critical thinking or via somewhat arbitrary lists of verbs and adverbs. We might call this a "mechanistic" approach to questioning.

Why doesn't the mechanistic approach work? Consider, for instance, a person who is just shown how to assemble a car engine from its parts. They learn that cylinders go here, torque this bolt to that setting, the pistons go here, the timing belt attaches here, and the starter motor goes here. But knowing all this doesn't necessarily mean he or she actually understands why or how the engine works.

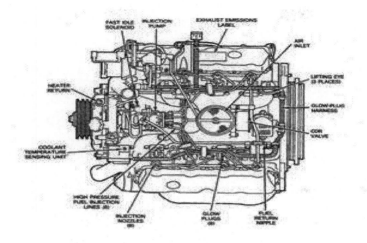

In fact, as I recount those very terms, I realize I hardly know anything about mechanical engines!

If the mechanistic-minded person were asked to fix a malfunctioning engine, he might not even know what part is responsible for doing a particular task. He could barely diagnose, let alone repair a malfunctioning engine--even though he might know how to assemble one entirely--because he doesn't deeply understand the way the engine actually works. Moreover, this same student certainly couldn't be expected to improve upon or create a better engine.

So I think it is very important that we invest in ourselves as teachers to acquire a deeper understanding as to why our framework for questioning is the way it is. We have to go well beyond simply accepting that we should ask questions in a way that parallels Bloom's Taxonomy just because Benjamin Bloom was a smart guy or that it just seems intuitively right to do so.

Why Good Questions Aren't Enough

The first thing we need to address is a common intuition that just asking questions--almost any questions--develops critical thinking skills. We might call this a 'just ask' framework: just ask questions and learning shall come. While I am a fan of questioning in general, just asking questions--even good ones--doesn't seem to correspond with developing critical thinking skills.

A situation in which lots of questions asked doesn't seem to equate with improved learning is when students take annual state tests. Most state tests ask a lot of questions. In just one of these exams, you might find 200 to 300 questions. That's a lot of questions. Moreover, the questions on these state exams range in difficulty from easy to intermediate to challenging. Inevitably, an exam will have at least some "good" questions on it.

The puzzling thing is, if there are both a range of questions and a multitude of questions being asked on these exams, why don't students seem to learn from this kind of questioning? I have never heard a student, after taking an exam say something like, "You know, your teaching over this past year was good; but that state exam, that really brought it all together for me! Now, I understand." If questions--and a quantity of questions at that--were all that it took to lead to learning, then just the experience of taking state exams year after year should improve learning.

I don't want to digress too much, but there are at least a few reasons why exam questions usually do not trigger learning, despite the many questions per exam. First, the questions are not contingent or patterned; question 15 doesn't depend on questions 14 or 13. Second, there is usually no need for students to justify in any detail a specific response--they just fill in an oval. Third, the process of taking an exam is usually not oral, and there are benefits to oral questioning and answering. Most of us "think" in language. The more we are prompted to articulate our thinking, the better our thinking may become.

Also, studies show that the average teachers asks many questions each day, perhaps up to 40,000 to 70,000 per year! So, if we are already asking lots of questions, then clearly it can't be that we're just not asking enough questions. There must be more to questioning than making sure we ask some "higher level" questions.

Using Questions To See Into the Mind

Instead of just asking good questions about our content, we need to change our focus to asking questions based upon the mental activity they are likely to trigger in our students. I call this "mind-focused" questioning. So we must shift our own thinking about the question we intend to ask from, "What do I want to ask about in the content?" to "What mental activity must I trigger in the student (via a question) to get him or her to understand the content?"

In English, we use certain verbs to describe the mental acts of thinking. We use words like labeling, comparing, sequencing, summarizing and so on. These words, when asked in a question, may trigger specific mental acts in the mind of the student. If we want a student to label something, we can ask him or her to "label" or "identify" or "find."

We do not have to always use the same verbs to engage the student in the mental act we want to trigger. We can use more natural language and get to the same result. We can ask, "What facts can you identify here?" or simply say, "Tell me what's going on here?" and in both cases, the student will probably label or identify something on the page.

On the other hand, when we don't use specific verbs, the student may end up comparing or inferring rather than labeling. Thus, our task is not satisfied by formalistically asking questions with certain verbiage. Use whatever words or verbs you want, just be sure they work to elicit the kind of mental activity you hope to see in the student.

It is equally important to listen the student's reply, so that you can infer what mental activity is actually going on in his or her head. Students will rarely tell you directly about their mental processing. When you ask them to infer, they probably won't reply with, "I infer that..." They will just give you their response, and you'll have to figure out what is going on inside his or her head. Is she inferring or really just still identifying or has she moved on to more of a summarization?

Mind-Focused v. Content-Focused Questioning

This core idea that questions should be used to trigger mental activity in the mind of the student might now seem obvious to you, but often this marks a big change in the way some educators have been taught to ask questions. When I ask some teachers to describe how they ask questions, they reply, "I ask questions about the content." From this mind-set, the questions we need to ask are natural to the content itself, almost obvious, inherent or self-evident.

Surely all content has its own structure and way of being looked at or understood. But there are a million, billion types of content out there. We must ask ourselves if the human brain was developed to specialize in each kind of physical or abstract phenomena that exists. Is there a brain--and a line of questions--for recognizing mountains and a different brain and line of questions for understanding math problems and yet another brain for music and a brain for understanding rare birds and a brain for comprehending the structure of atoms, which we didn't know even existed until recently in history? If our questions are uniquely framed from our content, then we are in a tough spot because of the multiplicity of fields of information out there. We would have to create a very specific line of questions for each kind of lesson to be taught.

The cognitive framework for questioning in this book does not assume that the student's brain comes with a mind wired for math or understanding great white sharks or the inner workings of a cell with a corresponding set of questions for each domain. Instead, this book proposed that there must be an algorithm for understanding in the brain for all content. By algorithm, I mean a process or a sequence for understanding a much wider range of content.

The algorithm my father developed for asking questions applies to all kinds of content. In many ways, it accords with Bloom's Taxonomy (as revised). And as you will later learn, it has five steps of questions associated towards understanding content and a two-step method for asking questions about assessment as implemented upon traditional multiple-choice questions/answers.

Forming a Scaffold of Mental Acts

The questions in this algorithm form a sort of 'cognitive scaffold', if you will. As educators, we mostly associate the term scaffolding with content or curriculum, such that a piece of content will lead to the next segment of content and skills build upon skills. In a similar sense, we ask questions that scaffold or build up the student's underlying mental acts of learning.

In the diagram above, imagine that each rung represents questions directed to a particular kind of mental act. This scaffold is organized well. It is ordered and has enough questions to lead the student to learning.

This next image shows questions that are in good cognitive order but infrequently asked; there simply aren't enough "foot holds" (i.e., questions) for the student to easily move up the scaffold. This implies that more questions tend to benefit students during questioning.

This third scaffold represents random questions that don't build upon each other; learning is notably sideways more so than upwards. This is what randomly asked questions look like.

Finally, this last scaffold represents infrequent questions that don't attend to the cognitive order of understanding. The student is bound to perceive the questions as episodic and not helpful towards learning. And as you can see, no one really gets anywhere, either.

In sum, it's important for us to ask questions to elicit mental activities from students in a particular order. That order doesn't have to be exact, in the sense that there is a precise order in which to ask 100 questions in a row. But we can say that some questions should be asked before others and that, even if any particular question might not have an exact place in that order, we should have a general idea of where it goes.

vs.

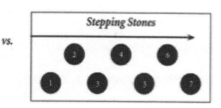

Another metaphor that may help to understand this need for ordering questions according to the mental acts they trigger is to imagine a series of stepping-stones across a river. I prefer this metaphor to the traditional metaphor of a stairway going upwards that is often used to represent the ascendency of thinking skills. The stairway metaphor makes it seem that the hardest thinking skills—and the hardest questions to ask and answer—are those at the highest levels. In fact, this may often be inaccurate. You may find that the hardest questions for your students are at the lower levels of thinking. Once those questions have been answered, often enough, the higher-level questions become much easier to consider, which seems counterintuitive.

The stepping-stones across of river metaphor is perhaps a more apt description of the ascendancy of thinking skills. In order to get to the opposing riverbank (your goal, whatever it may be), you need to cross the stones in some sort of order. You can't skip stones—thereby skipping certain mental acts—and expect to make it across. When we ask questions, if we skip eliciting certain mental activities, we may cause cognitive problems later down the line. For an obvious example, it is hard to compare something if you haven't labeled or identified the things to be compared, first.

In this sense, the "slipperiest" stone of thinking—the hardest question for the student—may be the first stone or instead the fifth, but not the last. Your first several questions may be more difficult for students than your last questions.

To this end, the stepping-stones metaphor communicates the need for order in questioning, and the realization that sometimes a "lower-level" question for comparison may be more difficult than an ostensibly "higher-level" question for synthesis or evaluation. Higher-level questions aren't necessarily harder to answer; they simply are later in place in the sequence of questioning.

Questioning and Bloom's Taxonomy

The reason I emphasize this idea of triggering mental acts in a particular (hierarchical) order is because some people have misapprehended how Bloom's Taxonomy relates to questioning strategies. The revised Bloom's Taxonomy is a very good device. It describes several levels of thinking that lead to what many people describe as critical thinking. But some educators think that they can simply "go to" the level of thinking they want and ask questions at that level without regard to what has occurred with their students in lower levels of thinking.

I've had administrators tell me that they want to emphasize higher-order questions while almost disregarding the fact that many of their students also have great difficulty with lower and middle order questions. These people make me think of encountering someone who is preparing to climb Mount Everest by climbing a hill near their house reasoning that it approximates the last 100 feet of the summit. That may be true, but Everest is a 29,000 foot mountain. You have to prepare to climb the whole thing!

When we perceive critical thinking more as an outcome and less as a process, our ability to ask questions effectively may suffer. Imagine a teacher who observes that a particular student shows a weakness in the ability to summarize information. Further imagine this teacher perceives that just asking more questions for summary is the correct solution. While this is a possibility, it is highly likely that the student may not be summarizing because of cognitive problems in lower domains, too. What if the student didn't find enough relationships or make enough comparisons within the content, lower levels of mental activity, to enable an accurate summary to be formed?

Thus, one common intuition perceives critical thinking skills as discrete acts that can be developed without consideration of the entire process. It imagines you can simply target areas of cognitive weakness independently. A different point of view, one that I present here, is that critical thinking is the entire process of developing mental acts in sequence. Referring back to the riverbank metaphor, it is the entire process of crossing all those stepping-stones in order. To others, critical thinking refers only to those higher-level mental acts or those final stones nearest the opposite riverbank.

Creating Expert Patterns of Thinking

In workshops, I often talk about two influential articles and a book that speak to this idea of the importance of creating patterns of mental activity. Both articles suggest that the ability to scaffold one's thoughts allows the expert learner to make predictions. Making predictions about the future is a hallmark of intelligence. One of the articles is, "Wayne Gretzsky-Style 'Field Sense' May Be Teachable" from May 22, 2007 in *Wired* magazine. The other is from *Scientific American*, "The Expert Mind," July 24, 2006.

In the *Wired* article, it described a scientist named Damian Farror from the Austrian Institute of Sport who constructed an elaborate experiment with high-ranking tennis players to assess whether it was reflex speed that made one player great, or simply very good. The outcome of the experiment was that it wasn't physical reflex speed that made one player return a serve better than another. The world's first-ranked tennis player wasn't often any faster than the twenty-fifth ranked player in terms of how far he could jump or how quickly he could run. Rather, it was the ability to anticipate where the ball was likely to go that made the great player move about one-third of a second sooner than the very good player. The great player is faster on the tennis court because his mind is quicker in predicting the future, not because his body is necessarily physically faster.

This realization always made me think of Michael Jordan, the basketball player. I would watch him play and he always seemed to be moving not just faster, but ahead of everyone else on the court. I knew he was a superb athlete, but I'm not sure Michael Jordan was always the fastest player on the court in terms of pure speed or the strongest. Rather, it makes sense that he was carving up the court almost magically because he was literally a bit ahead in time than the other amazing players of his day.

In the *Scientific American* article, a similar sort of experiment was done with chess players. It asked why some players became experts and others remained novices with both having played the game for the same amount of time.

Thinking in terms of school, we might ask the same question: Why do some students become experts after thirteen years of school and others, in the very same environment and with the same input of time, remain poor students? The conclusion of the *Scientific American* article again reflected that experts don't think faster or see many moves deeper into the game but seem to make better choices not so much on "an intrinsically stronger power of analysis as on a store of structured knowledge (emphasis on "structured")."

Both articles seem to imply that physical expertise or skill is a function of how the mind learns to see patterns on the chessboard or on the tennis court. But this same idea of developing patterns of thinking would appear to apply to abstract situations, too, like those found when reading text or examining a math problem in school. We need to develop patterns of thinking, but of what sort?

A Brain Algorithm

An influential book I discuss in workshops is by Jeff Hawkins and is titled, "On Intelligence" from 2006. To me, it provides the best explanation for why we must structure the questions we ask and gives a sense of how to do so. Hawkins proposes what he calls a memory-prediction theory of intelligence based on something called hierarchical-temporal memory and sparse distributed learning. It's a very deep book, so I can't do justice to it here, but I'll recount a few key ideas. I would also caution in advance that Jeff Hawkins' theory is exactly that, a theory, and one that regards how the human neocortex may function to construct intelligence.

In a beginning chapter, Hawkins recounts a key development in neuroscience. In the 1970s, a neuroscientist named Vernon Mountcastle made the observation that because the neocortex that envelops the brain looks the same all around, that perhaps there is a single common algorithm that makes the neocortex work. This was counter to the general proposition that the brain had different programs for each of its senses.

Experiments on rats suggested that Mountcastle's idea is true. In one experiment, it was shown that the nerve endings leading from the rat's eye to its brain can be connected to a different part of the neocortex and the rat will still learn to see, if not as well. If each form of stimuli required its own algorithm, it is unlikely you could connect the eyes nerve endings to a different part of the brain and end up with sight.

This idea that the brain is operating under a single algorithm is counterintuitive to most people because we perceive the world through our senses, leading us to confuse what the brain does with our senses themselves. The brain itself doesn't hear, see, smell or touch. In the brain there are no nerve endings and all stimuli is translated into electro-chemical impulses. Our senses, which seem so real to us, seem to end once they enter the brain.

So how can this algorithm of thinking be described? Hawkins's key insight is that the neocortex's algorithm is hierarchical in structure. By hierarchical, he doesn't mean that stimuli moves from the top layers of the neocortex to the bottom or up and down in terms of direction. He means that that information moves through the layers of the neocortex such that the thinking (or behavior therefrom) becomes increasingly abstracted over time, and this is fundamentally due to the way the neocortex is physically layered and connected.

While I have no evidence to confirm this, it would be an interesting symmetry that if the physical brain itself learns because of its hierarchical physical structure, leading from simple to abstract understandings, then our teaching should also be based on triggering mental acts in a hierarchical way. We would need to ask our questions in a pattern leading from simple to abstract understandings. We couldn't just ask good questions about the content; questions would be good based on how well they develop the hierarchical nature of the underlying content.

K-12 Implications of Hawkins' Theory

Hawkins' concept of the brain is also important for teachers because it gives us a sense of what "brain-based learning" should really mean. In education circles, there was a trend for many years to present teachers with information on the brain. Often, these seminars presented a sense of the brain as comprised of different components or functional areas.

Teachers were often told that scans of the brain made by functional magnetic resonance imaging (fMRIs) showed that information taken in via the eyes activates this part of the brain while information from the ears activates that part of the brain. Or that math content seems to touch here and poetry activates there. No doubt, there is truth to this presentation of the brain as doing different things in different places.

I'm not sure how knowing that one part of the brain is responsible for memory, while another part helps us to form language, actually helps us improve our instruction as teachers. What are you supposed to do with that information? If the parts of the brain activated by math are different than for history, and there is no underlying pattern for learning, then we can't really generalize an approach to understanding. But then, how does the brain—which is not programmed in advance for calculus and Chinese and poetry—think?

The Brain's Algorithm

An understanding of the brain that actually would give us guidance about how to teach would be of great service to us as instructors. It might also give us an overall approach on how to ask questions to our student. I think that Hawkins' book provides this pathway, even if he wasn't specifically addressing questioning strategies by K-12 teachers in his book.

As Hawkins' history of Lord Mountcastle recounts, while it is true that the brain processes different sorts of information in different parts of the neocortex, this is mostly an artifact of where the nerve endings happened to end up connecting to in the brain. The important thing isn't where exactly the nerve endings happen to connect within the neocortex. It's the fact that there may be a common algorithm at work across the brain.

Think about this! The idea that the brain is able to think and create intelligence because of something about the way it is structured—in a hierarchy. Hawkins believes that intelligence is an emergent property or expression of the hierarchical nature of underlying physiology of the physical brain.

Of course, just because the brain may be said to have some heretofore-unknown hierarchical system at the root of its capabilities, does not mean that we should disregard the uniqueness of each content area or of the senses themselves. Rather, as teachers, we must respect how each content area is unique and how the differing senses may help us understand. But we must also incorporate into our instructional approach the hierarchical patterns of learning required by the neocortex.

Hierarchical Thinking in Action

In one of my earliest versions of this book, which again was formerly titled, "Highly Effective Questioning," I used a thought experiment to suggest to readers how it is that our brains, though we perceive ourselves as seeing whole things or concepts at once, actually processes information in a sequential or hierarchical way over small increments of time.

To illustrate this, let me share the following images with you. It is important you spend just a bit of time with each image and answer the simple question: What do you see? I put just one image on each page on purpose, so that you don't see too much at once. What is this image?

When presented with the above image, some people will say it is a tail. Others say a paintbrush. Others say a root.

Let's go to the next image. Again, I've had to space the images out and waste a bit of paper, but it's better for you to take a moment really asking yourself, what do I see here?

PAGE INTENTIONALLY LEFT BLANK

So now what do you see? I won't make any suggestions. Just decide what this is.

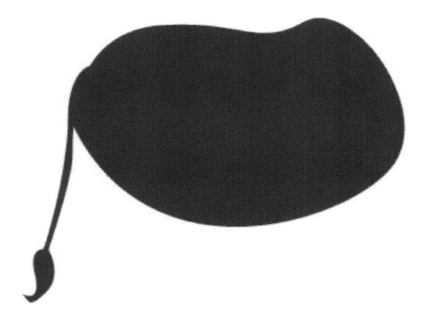

PAGE INTENTIONALLY LEFT BLANK

And what about now? What is this? What kind? Is there anything incongruent about it?

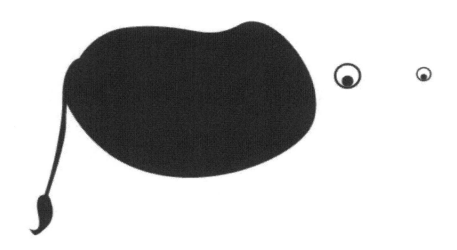

PAGE INTENTIONALLY LEFT BLANK

Ah-ha, you might think, there is an elephant. What about the other eye, though? And it is different, too.

Now the image is complete. But think back just a moment to the first image of the tail or paintbrush or whatever you thought it was. Did you immediately think "two elephants" or "family?" The concept wasn't there until your mind identified the pieces, figured out how they were connected, and eventually integrated enough connections so that your mind could create a summary.

Your mind operates in the same way when it looks at anything, from images of a couple of elephants to the lines and curves that make up letters that make up the words that make up the paragraphs that make up stories that give us ideas. Your mind goes from pieces to the whole; from content to concepts.

The futurist and inventor Ray Kurzweil has addressed the hierarchical nature of reality in his 2012 book called "How to Create a Mind," which references the earlier work of Jeff Hawkins. In "How to Create a Mind," Kurzweil says:

> *"The Web is itself a powerful and apt example of the ability of a hierarchical system to encompass a vast array of knowledge while preserving its inherent structure. The world itself is inherently hierarchical— trees contain branches; branches contain leaves; leaves contain veins. Buildings contain floors; floors contain rooms; rooms contain doorways, windows, walls, and floors."*

Kurzweil's ambition is far greater than merely changing how we teach. He believes we will soon create truly thinking machines whose ability to think will emerge from their inherently hierarchical organization of connected parts. Kurzweil now works at Google, incidentally. And Jeff Hawkins' company, Numenta, seems to be making significant advances in computer learning via brain-based algorithms.

My goal in this book is not nearly so ambitious. For the limited purpose of this book, we can now summarize our cognitive approach to questioning as this: Our questions should focus on constructing a hierarchical pattern of mental activity, an algorithm, in the mind of the student across all kinds of content so that she or he can form expert patterns and become independent in his or her thinking. We must plan and ask our questions in hierarchical patterns.

APPLICATION

We want to construct a pattern of questions that reliably leads to learning. Let's take an overview of how our cognitive framework of questions applies to the lessons we commonly see in textbooks or even on tests.

Our pedagogy has seven types of questions we use to trigger mental acts in sequence. Because the types of questions are in an order and lead into each other, I call them "steps" most of the time.

The questions are divided into two categories. Five of the steps are questions that elicit mental activity when looking at what we would call "content." This of course is the information we want to the students to learn. The other two steps are questions that elicit mental activity when looking at "assessment." Assessment is the part of a lesson where some form of examination of what was learned occurs (the "test" part). The content steps are steps 1 to 5 and assessment steps are Q and A.

Content Questions

Step 1 questions are for labeling and identification of relevant facts.

Step 2 questions are for comparing, inferring and making connections or disconnections.

Step 3 questions are for ordering and making short summaries.

Step 4 questions are for application, prediction and change.

Step 5 questions are for making meta-summaries, reflection and setting goals.

In the graphic below, you can see a selection of "content" about a firework. The content includes the title, the text, and the diagram of the rocket itself. Our questions in Steps 1-5 would elicit the corresponding cognitive acts about the text and the picture given.

Fireworks

Fireworks displays are often associated with celebrations. Some fireworks are rockets that can be fired into the air, producing colorful patterns of bright light. One rocket design involves a cardboard tube, a propellant, and a fuse. A cap on the tube contains metal salts and explosive powder with a second fuse. The propellant consists of a mixture of carbon (C), sulfur (S), and potassium nitrate (KNO_3). Potassium nitrate is a potassium ion (K^+) bonded to a nitrate ion (NO_3^-).

A long cardboard tube is filled with the propellant. When a lit fuse ignites the propellant, the propellant releases oxygen, produces flames, and forces gas out the bottom of the rocket. These actions cause the rocket to rise high into the air.

As the rocket reaches its maximum height, a second fuse ignites an explosion that heats and burns the metal salts. This heating and burning of metal salts produces large colorful flashes. Many people enjoy watching these colorful displays against the night sky.

The use of fireworks can be dangerous. Professionals who use fireworks take many safety precautions while setting up and igniting the displays.

Firework Rocket Design

Assessment Questions

Step Q questions are for interpretation and justification of test queries.

Step A questions are for answering and justifying selected or constructed answers.

The graphic that follows has four questions that form the assessment section of the lesson. Thus, there could be four instances of Step Q, where we ask students to examine test prompts. Also, there could be at least four instances of Step A, where we ask students to select an answer-choice and then justify that selection. If students do not initially select the correct-answer and justify it properly, obviously you will need to repeat your Step A several times.

17 Which of the following information would allow the most direct calculation of the average speed of the rocket on its upward flight?

A   Thrust force and wind speed

B   Maximum height and the time it takes the rocket to reach it

C   Rocket mass and the time it takes the rocket to reach the highest point

D   Thrust force and the time it takes the rocket to fall to the ground

19 When the fuse ignites the contents of a firework, oxygen is consumed as a result of which type of change?

A   Mass

B   Phase

C   Nuclear

D   Chemical

18 As a rocket rises, its kinetic energy changes. At the time the rocket reaches its highest point, most of the kinetic energy of the rocket has been —

F   permanently destroyed

G   transformed into potential energy

H   converted to friction

J   stored in bonds between its atoms

20 A scientist hypothesizes that the use of a propellant other than the traditional mixture of C, S, and KNO_3 will cause a rocket to rise higher into the air. The researcher builds a rocket that uses an alternate propellant. A proper control for the experiment would be an identical rocket that uses —

F   the traditional propellant

G   the alternate propellant

H   no propellants

J   a mixture of both propellants

Following the Cognitive Scaffold of Questions

Although we do encourage following the overall sequence of questions, please remember that we may focus on a particular step(s) of questioning as needed. Perhaps our class of students may be proficient answering questions for labeling (step 1) but not for finding connections (step 2). In that event, we can focus more of your questions on step 2 and fewer in step 1. Don't forget to try to always ask at least some questions in every step of the questioning process or we might find ourselves with holes in the cognitive scaffold.

Remember that although we do plan to ask questions in a particular order, this is not an exact science. Different people will perceive some questions as fitting into one step whereas others will feel they serve to elicit a different cognitive act. So we say only that our questioning is organized but not exact. It's like a road map of questions; there is no GPS coordinate for each question, only a general place.

Before You Start: Have an End-Goal for the Questioning

Before we begin to look at each of the seven steps of questioning, please keep in mind that our questions must have a final goal in mind. The questions we ask must lead to the development of a particular idea. I've seen a teacher ask questions in a seemingly good cognitive order, but have no overall point for questioning, no goal.

In one classroom observation, I saw an elementary teacher dutifully ask questions that scaffolded up the content (steps 1-5) very nicely using a short written dialogue for the lesson. Though I was glad to see that she organized her questions very well, there seemed something amiss. I asked her, "What was your overall goal in this lesson? What were you trying to teach?"

She quickly replied that she was trying to teach how punctuation affected our understanding of the characters' feelings. So I next asked her, "How many of your questions attended to punctuation?" Her face went white, and she realized that if that indeed was the goal of her teaching, then her questions weren't directed towards that goal. In fact, I'm not so sure that what she said was actually her goal, as the story really didn't even have a lot of meaningfully different punctuation to create nuances in character. But again, if that was in fact her goal, then all her well-scaffolded questions weren't leading to that particular goal.

So, the point is, ask yourself, "What do I want my students to know here?" before you start creating and organizing your questions. Decide your purpose, and then create the scaffold of questions that will develop that with your students. I find it helpful to write an explicit goal for my questioning in addition to the questions themselves: "I am asking these questions so that the students will" and fill in the rest.

The Imagined Conversation

Ultimately, thinking through the questions you intend to ask (based on a scaffold of mental acts) and contemplating the students' likely answers or responses (convergent or divergent) helps to form what I can an "imagined conversation." Although the actual conversation that ends up occurring isn't going to be 100% a simulacrum of what you had planned, it's going to make it a lot easier to deal with divergent answers because you will probably have another question "in your pocket" at the ready. That is, because you've planned and thought through things, you will be ready to correct them without getting flustered or not knowing what to ask next.

Remember, then, that the purpose of all this sequential, premeditated questioning isn't just to create inputs and hear appropriate outputs, like some sort of machine process. No, it's about engaging the minds of your students and hearing their understandings of reality, respecting that somehow, this universe has conspired all this moment to give us the opportunity to engage each other. It can be pretty cool.

With all this now said, let's get to the steps of questions.

STEP ONE

We begin our questioning having assumed that our students have already been exposed to the underlying content (book, article, graphic, problem, concept, et cetera). Hopefully, they have already read or reviewed or watched something about which we are going to base most of our questions. But sometimes, we will have to ask questions and expose students to the content at the same time.

So what are Step 1 questions? Step 1 questions ask students to label, identify or find relevant information and facts form the page, unit, chapter, problem, video or whatever is your content. There are other verbs that will get the job done. You may ask students to look, notice, see, examine or name. You may use more natural language rather than sounding very rigid by asking students, "What's going on here (in the content)?" and hopefully that will trigger the proper mental activity. Step 1 questions are often (but not always) generated by the adverbs who, what, where and when.

Step 1 questions have sometimes been labeled as "knowledge-level" questions in education training. It is true that Step 1 questions clearly target a lower-level thinking skill. But this thinking skill is still a critical thinking skill. If we skip asking questions in this step altogether, or if we don't ask enough questions, we may leave holes in the ladder of thinking.

A student who fails to label or identify relevant information in the content may not be able to make connections or summarize properly in succeeding stages of questioning. It is a good practice to ask at least some of Step 1 questions to ensure that all students have a grasp of the basic facts, even if we would prefer to ask most of our questions at higher levels of thinking. Don't get stuck at this step, but don't forget to pay some attention here, either.

Be aware that although some questions may sound like they are lower-level questions aligned for Step 1, just because they use an adverb like "what" or a verb like "identify," doesn't mean they are actually Step 1 questions. Consider a question like, "Who is the main character of this story?" People sometimes think that because it uses the adverb "who," it is a Step 1 question. But cognitively, that question seems to ask more for an inference or perhaps even a summary or synthesis of who the primary character could be amongst several characters. In this way, the question is more similar to "What is the main idea of the story?" which is more obviously not a Step 1 question. In short, keep your focus on the cognitive act being triggered, not the verbs or adverbs being employed.

Cognitive Roadblock: Indiscriminate Labeling

You might think that asking questions at this stage would be uneventful and mostly responded to with success. The questions seem pretty easy. In my experience, many underachieving students have problems answering even these Step 1 kinds of questions for identification of information.

When I began my work in questioning years ago, during live student demos, I was often puzzled when some students would have trouble with these initial questions. They seemed so simple. And if the students were having trouble with these easy questions, what did this portend for other, more difficult questions I wanted to ask them later?

It wasn't that these students couldn't answer these questions at all. They usually were able to label or identify things, but they would often pick out irrelevant facts as often as relevant ones. It was like they would just pick a spot on the page and give a response from that. Their labeling and identification was indiscriminate.

What I came to understand is that these students were seeing the information on the page in an episodic way. They could label or find information, but not systematically. In particular, they did not discriminate between relevant and irrelevant facts. The information was unfiltered.

Oppositely, students who were more successful in answering Step 1 questions looked at the information or content differently. They had patterns of thinking even for basic facts or information. They approached information on a page or in a video or in a lecture looking for relevancy even when taking in the most basic information.

In fact, I later learned that studies have been done to track the rapid eye movements, known as "saccades" of students as they observed a lesson. (I believe this has also been done in sports to ascertain what the great players see). The patterns of the lower-performing students are more random. The patterns of higher-performing students tend to see relevant information, first, and spend more time on the relevant information altogether.

Thus, to help all students internalize a better pattern of searching for basic facts, we include the concept of relevancy in our questions even at this easiest stage of questioning. We ask, "Can you label the KEY information?" or "What are the MOST IMPORTANT facts of the story?" or "Where should we BEGIN to look for relevant facts?"

Notice that the mental acts are still labeling and identifying, but there is a stress towards discriminating amongst all the things to be labeled or identified. I describe this rule of asking students to label or identify with an attention towards relevancy. Our slogan might be "Relevant Facts First!"

Thus, we should ask students to notice the information in its order of relevancy. For example, if the title to a passage of text is a relevant fact, and it almost always is, we should ask them about the title right away. Don't ask about the title with your twentieth question. Underachieving students may need to be prompted to look at the title with your first few questions, consistently, so they learn a key rule of identifying the title right away.

In math, if the order of operations is always operant, ask your students questions with that in mind, "Where must we begin to look at things in this equation?" If you are studying social studies and reference a chart with a legend, ask questions about the legend sooner rather than later if it contains highly relevant information. As you may perceive, every kind of content has its own order of relevancy.

In workshops, I tell a story about when I went to a batting cage and tried to hit some fast pitch balls. I had no chance. But there must be something that a professional baseball player does to give himself a chance of hitting the ball. Those things are completely lost on me, but I'm sure that the batter is focusing on just a few key things to give him a sense of the coming pitch. As a lawyer, I often look for very specific things when listening to the facts of a case, which help me assess whether it is worth pursuing. Lawyer, baseball player, student—each has its own way of "seeing" the basic facts that require one's attention.

Applying this strategy in the classroom may change the way we ask students to look for basic facts. Take a common scenario. Imagine students at an elementary level who have a selection of text in front of them with many highlighted or bold-faced words. You'll often hear a teacher begin by asking, "So, what does this word mean? What does that term mean?" This might seem like good questioning for labeling because there are many unknown words on the page.

There is nothing wrong with asking students to define unknown terms or words. But we have to consider that we are setting a pattern for the future with our questions. Do we want to teach students to try to define unknown words as the first thing they should do when they look at a page of text? Is that how we actually read a newspaper or a book? Or do we really label things as we go along while searching for more relevant cues?

I don't have a set formula to help us distinguish between better or worse questions for Step 1, but a question I ask myself before starting is, "How do I want them to see this information not just for now, but for the future?"

Why Relevancy Isn't Automatic

A deeper puzzle is why students don't naturally see relevant information rather than irrelevant information. Good students naturally seem to pick out relevant rather than irrelevant facts. Why don't all students do this? Why doesn't experience teach the idea of relevancy?

My explanation is that even though relevant facts may seem obvious or self-evident to us, many learners do not notice the relevant information because there is no inherent feedback mechanism. This lack of a feedback mechanism develops into a cognitive roadblock for some students.

In regular life, the physical world always gives us feedback about what is relevant or not relevant. If we don't see a chair or a banana peel on the floor, we soon learn about them. No one has to tell us to turn on a light switch when entering a darkened room because we've all surely run into something in the dark—and it hurts!

But the content of school is fundamentally different than our experience with physical things. School is inherently abstract. Even the basic facts of a story are still abstract. They don't really exist except in your head. If a student overlooks some important information on a page of a book, the textbook doesn't correct him. For all the highlights and colors and annotations, they just don't mean much if the student isn't looking for them in the first place. Maybe one day the textbooks will follow our eyes and prompt us if we skip something, but that's the future. As I say in workshops, the content of school is a often literally flat—there is no obvious topography from which to infer what is most important to label or identify, first.

Speaking of textbooks, some do a fine job of presenting information in consistent ways. But some textbooks present information in a mish-mash of pictures, text, colors and lines. I've seen textbooks where the color red, which is traditionally associated with a correction or warning is used with seemingly no rationale or pattern. Sometimes pictures are only tangentially related to the concept being taught. In a way, textbooks like these can scatter the underachieving student's thinking process. They learn to see everything and, therefore, sort of nothing.

This means that depending on the way your content is presented in the textbook, you might have to work extra hard to use questions to guide the students to the relevant facts or information during this first step of asking questions.

STEP TWO

After we have asked students to find, notice or see the relevant facts in the content, it is time to ask questions that elicit connections between those same pieces of information. We may use verbs like compare, connect, contrast, and infer. We may also find ourselves using the adverbs how and why quite a bit to initiate these questions.

The purpose of questions in Step 2 is to create linkages for a chain of understanding. The goal is to get students to connect pieces of information together by cause and effect, sequence, logic, relationship and so forth. At a minimum, ask students to connect some of the things they identified back in Step 1.

Some examples of Step 2 questions might be, "Can you compare this character to that one?" or "How does this paragraph lead to the next paragraph?" or "How do you go from line 4 of the math problem to line 5?" or "What is the relationship between this cellular structure and the functioning of the cell?"

Be careful not to assume that just because you have asked a question with 'how' or 'why' that the question will elicit connection or comparison or inference. A question like, "How did John get to the town?" probably asks more for identification (Step 1) than for connection if the answer is "John arrived by train."

When asking Step 2 kinds of questions, some teachers end up asking more concrete questions. For instance, questions that ask students to compare two characters are fairly easy to ask, because the subjects of the comparison are usually easily defined. Less frequently, do we ask questions that require comparison of complex wholes. For instance, asking a student, "How does paragraph/chapter 2 develop what was learned in paragraph/chapter 1" is measurably harder than asking, "How are John and Bill the same?" My suggestion here is only to be sure that some of your questions in Step 2 reach for connections that encompass larger amounts of content than the more obvious "one to one" comparisons or connections that often come to mind. In short, make your questions for comparison broader or deeper.

Cognitive Roadblock: Avoiding Disconnections

Within this second step of questions is a subset of questions that students often have more difficulty answering. These are questions that seek to elicit a disconnection between facts or assess the strength or weakness of a connection. It's when we ask, "Does the author prove her point in the next paragraph?" and the desired response is, "Not really, because she doesn't..." Or when you ask, "Does anything seem wrong here?" hoping students will infer some error. It's when we ask students to notice that something in a math problem is not needed ("disconnected") from our task so that the best response from the student is, "No, that isn't needed because we're looking for kilos and what that says is kilometers."

There is a particular benefit to asking questions that elicit disconnections while examining content. That benefit culminates during assessment. In most lessons, after the content comes a section for assessment in the form of written questions and multiple-choice answers. Each question is usually followed by four answer-choices.

In most multiple-choice queries, three of the four answer-choices are incorrect. The reason an answer-choice is incorrect is often because it is disconnected from either the content or the question being asked. Put simply, answer-choice "C" might be incorrect because it can't be found in the content or doesn't answer the written question. It is disconnected.

Asking more disconnection questions while evaluating the content helps students later with the assessment section, when they must examine multiple-choice answers and know what makes something wrong or disconnected.

Risking the True Narrative

An interesting question for us to consider is why some teachers tend to avoid asking disconnection questions but are happy to ask other kinds of Step 2 questions? They are happy to ask, "What is the relationship between paragraph 1 and the information in the chart" but won't ask, "Why did the author make that his title" if the best response from the student should be, "I'm not really sure that is a good title." Put another way, why do some of us feel uncomfortable with asking students to notice flaws in content.

I think one possibility may be that as teachers, we subconsciously want to create what I call "true narratives" about whatever it is we teach. A true narrative is the sense that the information we show our students or is in the book or on the chart is true, accurate, impartial and complete.

We may worry that if students perceive their content as having some faults, that they won't see the larger picture of truth in the information. For instance, maybe a story is poorly written. We may avoid asking questions that would leave the students critical of the author or writing itself.

This tendency to avoid risking the true narrative applies equally to other modalities of instruction, such as lecture. We normally want to tell our students that something makes sense and not that it has weaknesses, flaws, or problems.

One domain that highlights in a very concrete way our adherence to the "true narrative" is in some math textbooks, or certainly the ones I used to see when I was a student. Usually, at the beginning of a math unit or section, you'll see a sample problem or two, and it was always properly solved. Then, after those two perfect examples, you'd get a series of problems to solve.

What was very rare, in my own education (granted, in the 1980s), was that you would hardly ever see examples showing the most common errors broken down in a step-by-step way. Which is really sort of bizarre, given that in math, there are often just a few common errors for a certain type of problem beyond pure computational errors.

It seems like it would be pretty easy to say, "Here's the right way to solve this. And here are three examples showing the most common mistakes made, and how they are made." My point here isn't to critique mathematics textbooks, but to suggest that this idea of true narrative is a real thing, and that we often sidestep away from asking "disconnecting" questions.

In workshops, teachers often ask me the following question in regards to the concept of disconnection or error: "If I ask (or tell) students about errors in the content, aren't the students likely to think the error is true or correct? For instance, if I ask a student to explain an answer that they believe is correct but I know is incorrect, and they go on to do so, couldn't that leave them with a misimpression that they are correct? Won't that reinforce the error? Or what if I ask them about a statement in a story that can't be connected to anything. Won't they discount the whole story?"

My response is that I believe students need to realize that questions don't always seek to make connections or show something true; questions can just as easily be used to point out fallacies, weaknesses, errors and disconnections. Cue Jack Nicholson yelling, "You can't handle the truth!" from the movie A Few Good Men. We fear that if we show students (or ask, hopefully) about errors, we will invite that same error. I don't think that is true any more than asking someone about an underinflated tire is likely to make the tire any more flat.

If we remain aware to ask both step one labeling questions and step two connection/disconnection questions, we create a basic foundation of understanding. We help students to exercise some essential cognitive functions requisite to higher level thinking skills. And we overcome a cognitive roadblock by helping students assess the strengths and weaknesses in the content in front of them.

STEP THREE

Our third step of questions helps students put things together and begins to make generalizations, see themes and notice patterns. After our students have labeled facts (Step 1) and found connections between some of the information (Step 2), we ask questions that elicit short summaries or outlines of the information in chunks.

Imagine your students have gone through a few pages or paragraphs of information. Or perhaps they are looking at a long math problem with ten lines of operations. We might ask, "Can you summarize for me what happened on the first page?" or "What is the sequence for the first five operations we need to do here?" Just as before, we may be more general in our language. We may ask, "What's going on so far?" or "What's this all about?" or "Put this all together for me up to this point?"

These short summaries ask students to integrate information as they go along. They are distinguished from a single, final summary at the end of a unit or chapter or topic because they cover less ground and entail less personal reflection. Obviously, the teacher has to decide when enough information has been covered to warrant a recap.

I prefer to think of this step as more outlining or ordering than summary. What's the difference? Well, many students have internalized a rule that to summarize means to "put things together in ten words or less." In fact, that's often the exact wording they'll give if I ask them what a summary means. I think this response comes from the world of taking too many exams, perhaps.

Outlining is a better way of framing what we are seeking here through our third step of questions. An outline of a selection of text might be as simple as beginning, middle, and end. An outline highlights key points. I'd rather students outline several key points of a selection of text or a timeline than to merely put the whole selection in "ten words or less." For whatever reason, the use of the verb "outline" seems to result in a better short summary than the use of the word "summary" itself. In fact, maybe the best verb to reply upon is order. Can you put this in order? What is the order here? And so on. Whether you use order, organize, or a different set of language, the idea is for students to gather the information into a larger pattern.

Also, note that the responses given by the students should take some time to vocalize. There is no set rule here, but if the response is wholly given in less than a few seconds, then the amount of summary being done is too little. When I demonstrate with students, I like to have them summarize or order and expect them to talk for at least 20-30 seconds or more.

Questions that elicit summary often appear on state tests, even if they don't always explicitly use the word summary in the test questions. For example, a common test question in reading comprehension asks, "What is the main idea of the story?" In order to answer that question, the student must be able to tell what the story was about from beginning to end. Another question, "Which title best represents...?" requires that the student be able to summarize the content and select the title that best represents it. A question like, "Which equation would you use?" is another example of a question seeking a summation, because it requires students to "see through" to the end of a process and select the appropriate equation.

Cognitive Roadblock: Passing the Baton

One common roadblock in this step is something I call "passing the baton." It's not so much a cognitive problem as what some teachers naturally do when asking questions for summary. If you've ever seen a relay race, you know that no single person completes the whole race. A baton or stick is passed from one person to another to another until the entire distance is traversed.

This may also happen when we ask Step 3 questions. Instead of asking a single student to summarize or outline the whole of something, we may do something like this: "John, can you tell me about A?" and then "Mary, can you tell me about part B?" and "Sam, what happened in part C?" If the students answer correctly, intuitively it may feel like a summary has been achieved because all the parts of the content have been mentioned. But no single student has actually done a complete summary of A, B and C.

There may be a good reason to split-up the summary amongst several students. For one thing, we may want to get more students to participate, which is a good intention. However, by doing so, we diminish the amount of summary each student actually ends up doing. We must strike a balance here.

Another consideration might be that we fear that when a student talks for too long in attempting to summarize something, the other students will tune out. If John talks for a minute while attempting to summarize, how do we control the attention of Mary and Sam? To help with this, you may tell students in advance that they may "cheat" off the previous summaries they hear.

Going back to our example, it would be better to ask, "John, tell me about A, B and C?" and then say, "Mary, you heard what John said, so now tell me about A, B, and C in your own way?" But take note, don't allow students to just say, "Uh, what she said." If a student says that, say, "Okay, then, exactly what did she say?"

In workshops, I tell a story about how these first three steps of questioning really can make a difference not only in academics, but even in regular life. A year ago, I had to attempt several home remodeling projects. Fortunately, my friend, Chris was a really hard worker. We would barely start the day and he'd just want to rush out and buy the materials required for that day's project. But I noticed that we kept missing items or got the wrong ones and so I was going to the hardware store several times in a day. It was clear we needed more structure.

I started out by asking Chris questions to identify and label the tools or materials we'd need for the tasks at hand. Each day, we created a list of those things before we went to the store. We started going to the store less often.

I then noticed that sometimes, we'd have something on the list and get back to the project only to find it was missing a related item. To put it simply, we'd go and get a hammer only to find we were missing nails. So, I started to ask Chris how each item on the list was related to the project or what it needed it function--making connections. One time, I asked Chris why he needed a particular tool and he eventually had to admit that it wasn't related to anything, he just wanted it. That was what I call a question that found a disconnection!

As you might guess, we became much more efficient, but I found that asking Chris to make a short summary of what he intended to do each day helped to organize our projects even better. He'd sometimes change the order of the day after thinking it through.

The three steps of questions took some time to ask. Chris was mostly used to just start working, not thinking through the tasks of a project sequentially. I think the questions not only saved me time and money, they changed the way Chris thought about how to approach his work.

STEP FOUR

After we have made some short summaries and assuming there is no need to answer written test questions, we continue our examination of the content and ask students to apply, predict, or assume a change in the underlying information.

Questions in this fourth step are based on the idea of some sort of change in the content and the outcomes of that change. For example, we might ask, "How would the outcome have been different if this change had/had not happened?" Or "What would happen if X were made negative?"

Interestingly, these kinds of questions are less common on state tests, though they certainly do develop higher-level critical thinking skills. One explanation for their scarcity on tests might be that when you ask students to make predictions, the scope of reasonable answers becomes larger. If you ask, "According to the story, what is likely to happen?" it becomes harder to have only a single, correct answer.

Cognitive Roadblock: Predicting Before Knowing

Questions that ask students to make changes or assume new facts in or about the content should be asked later in the sequence of questions. The cognitive roadblock is when we ask these questions without laying a foundation of questions in the earlier cognitive steps.

It's hard to properly answer a question like, "How would the story be different" if you are unable to answer, "What were the key facts of the story?" or "What is a good summary of the information?" Predicting without knowing is skipping some significant cognitive operations; it's like trying to leap most of the way across the river of content. If a good foundation has been set through previous questions, these questions for prediction and application should be fun to consider rather than difficult.

Though I wouldn't call the following a cognitive roadblock, it is something to consider. In reading comprehension, this fourth step of questions is often put this way, "What would you have done if..." It seeks to get students to project themselves into the content. This isn't bad. But it's a lower kind of Step 4 question than asking something like, "How would you change the story to include yourself in it?"

This is just to say that the idea of projection is a little bit less cognitively demanding, in my opinion, than asking students to make a change in the underlying content and discover the implications of that change. My preferred way of creating these kinds of questions is to think of the idea of making a change in things and asking the students about that.

STEP FIVE

The last step of our content questions asks students to make a final summary of the learning. We dedicate a few queries at the end of our instructional segment dedicated to questioning to elicit a meta-summary from students. We ask, "What was learned overall today?" or "Did we meet our goals?"

Questions in Step 5 may also elicit a more regular summary of the underlying content, "What was this story all about, again?" or "What were the five key points we learned today?" But the goal is to bridge from a summary of the content to itself to a summary of the learning achieved.

We must assume that students who cannot answer, "What did we learn today?" in some way leave the room not knowing exactly what they did or what was accomplished. They may know pieces of content, but it's unlikely they see the overall instructional theme. As I say in workshops, "For them, it's as if Wednesday could just as easily come before Tuesday. The instruction doesn't flow together because aren't putting it all together."

Cognitive Roadblock: Doing the Summary Yourself

In the rush of the last few minutes of a class period or an instructional segment dedicated to asking questions, we sometimes may unintentionally do much of the meta-summary for students. The teacher will be at the front of the room, saying, "Okay, today, we did X and Y. Tomorrow, we're going to do Z." Better for students to tell us what they did today, leaving us to tell them what tomorrow is going to hold.

So, be sure to give students the chance to answer even a few reflective questions at the end of your instruction. This helps students to see that instruction is moving along a path, not just episodically going this way or that.

STEP Q

The first five steps of questioning help students to develop a pattern of thinking when analyzing content. These questions ask students to find relevant facts (step 1), make connections between them (step 2), develop frequent short summaries (step 3), consider the effects of changes to the content (step 4) and make a final summary of the learning (step 5). Now, let's move on to the questions we might ask about assessment. Not all content comes with a follow-up assessment section, but many do. Steps Q and A help us to ask questions about written questions usually found in the assessment section of the unit. The assessment segment usually follows the content.

Step Q is a framework for engaging students at the level of the test question. In step Q, we follow something we call the RIJ sequence. We first ask a student to *read* the written question. Then, we ask students to *interpret* the written question. Finally, we ask students to *justify* their interpretation of the written question. Note that we are not asking students to justify the "answer" to the question, yet. We are just asking for a justification of their initial interpretation of the question itself.

Consider the following question and let's apply the RIJ framework to it.

Q. What is the best generalization of the author's attitude towards the main character of the story?

     Answer A

     Answer B

     Answer C

     Answer D

Following the RIJ sequence, we need to ask:

Read: Can someone read the question?

Interpret: What is the question asking?

Justify: Why do you think the question asks us that?

The process seems simple. But it doesn't always go as planned. Consider this script of the RIJ process at work.

Teacher: So, can someone read the question? How about you, David?

Student: What is the best....generalization of the...author's attitude towards the main character?

Teacher: Fine. What is the question asking? Samantha?

Student: It's asking, what is the best generalization of the author's attitude of the main character?

Teacher: Okay. But I need you to actually interpret the question. What is the question asking us, Samantha?

Student: It's asking what is, um, the best overall, what is my opinion overall of the main character.

Teacher: Okay. Why do you think the question asks you that?

Notice in this sample script that the student initially just reads the question back. Then, when she does give an interpretation she actually misinterprets what the question is asking. Here, the teacher doesn't stop and say, "No, that's not what the question is asking." The teacher continues in a neutral way and asks the student to justify her interpretation of the question.

Samantha probably will struggle to justify her interpretation. The teacher should attempt to correct Samantha's misinterpretation with a few more questions. Those corrective questions are up to the teacher. They may ask the student to re-read the question or label key words in the question or establish connections in the question or compare the question to other questions they have seen and so on. There is no single strategy for engaging in corrective action, though we can sort of use the cognitive scaffold as a guide.

But please note that we reserve "corrective action" for after the RIJ process. We want students to at least invest some effort into independently understanding the question and not just to wait for our corrective action as a guide. The benefit of the RIJ strategy preceding corrective action is that it puts the initial work of interpreting test questions onto the student. It says to students, I assume you can read and interpret with reasoning or evidence what you think a question is asking you to do, answer, find or solve. I don't mind helping you to understand a question if you don't understand it (i.e., corrective action), but you will have to put a down-payment on the question with the RIJ strategy before I will start helping you.

We want students to start thinking to themselves, "Let me read this question. What's it asking? How do I know that?" Perhaps a way of outlining our approach is to add the corrective action after the RIJ so that it looks like this:

Read

Interpret

Justify

Corrective Action

Few Truly New Test Questions

You may wonder why our strategy in step Q breaks away from the five steps of questioning dedicated to understanding content. Why don't we ask students to label, compare, summarize, apply and re-summarize the test question? This is because when students are learning new content, the first five steps of cognitive acts are needed for understanding. But most test questions are not really new "content" to students.

Many test questions stay the same year after year. In first grade, you'll see a question that says, "What was this story all about?" In sixth grade, it might be phrased as, "What is the main idea of the story?" In tenth grade, it could be, "Select the best summary of the story." Many test questions aren't really new to students after a certain age.

If we treat test questions like they are always new to the student, we create an incentive structure wherein students will learn to wait for the teacher to prompt them through every detail of a question. They learn not to invest effort initially and expect corrective action as the starting point. They come to expect the teacher to lead them through a test question that has possibly just 10 to 40 words the same as if they were being led through a 10 to 40 page chapter in a novel. In short, treating assessment like content makes students mentally lazy.

So, the RIJ framework differs from the step 1-5 framework on purpose. We shift gears and recognize that questions to elicit understanding of content should differ from the way we ask questions about assessment.

Cognitive Roadblock: Too Many Patterns

Most teachers have not been given a framework for asking students to analyze test questions, which is an odd thing, I think. For most teachers, we subconsciously imitate how we remember being asked to look at test questions or just go by our own intuition. A consequence of this varied approach is that students end up analyzing test questions according to several different patterns. They may not develop a consistent framework for understanding test queries.

Below are some examples of different ways of asking students about test questions. It's not that any one of these patterns is necessarily a bad way of approaching a test question. But the mixture of many varying patterns surely must create a sense that every written test question is a question of first impression. Again, this may hinder some students from developing a reliable pattern—in our case, the RIJ approach—to help them examine a test question.

Skips Question, Looks at Answers

This pattern is when the teacher says, "Okay, read the question. Now, what answer do you select to eliminate?" Here, the teacher has skipped any interpretation of the question.

Teacher Reads and Asks for Interpretation

"I'm going to read the question for you, 'What is the best expression of a reasonable inference that can be made about the author?' So, what is the question asking us?" Rather than asking a student to read the question, the teacher does it for his or her students.

Interprets Question for Students

This is when the teacher says, "So, it's asking what the product, which means multiply, what the product would be if you multiplied two negative numbers..." Here, the teacher does most of the interpretation of the question.

Fails to Ask for Justification of the Interpretation

A student is asked to read and interpret a question. Then the teacher says, "That's right, that's what the question asks. So, what is your answer?" Here, the teacher only affirms that the interpretation of the question is correct. We don't learn why it is correct.

Treats the Question Like Content

The teacher asks students to look at the question. "So, what does the word 'perimeter' mean in the question? What does the term closed-figure mean? What is the relationship between those two terms?" Here, the teacher starts breaking down the question--a corrective action approach-- without first having given an opportunity to RIJ the question. The teacher thus takes the work out of the question. When the student sees a similar question, that student may likely forget she ever saw it because the most or all the work was initially prompted by the teacher.

STEP A

After students have properly interpreted what the written assessment question is asking, it's now time to look at the answers. If the question is constructed response, then ask your students to write out their response and then justify it. But if the question is multiple-choice, we have some other things to consider.

In a multiple-choice question, we ask students to read all answer-choices, select the best one and be prepared to justify that selection. Pretty simple. It might sound something like this:

Teacher: Please read all the answer-choices.

Teacher: Now, select the best possible answer, the one that answers the question being asked.

Student: I select C.

Teacher: What does C say? Why do you select C?

Answer-choice C might be correct or incorrect. Either way, the student is asked to justify that selection.

If the student has selected an incorrect response and gets stuck in the process of justifying that selection, there are two things to remember as you try to guide them to understanding. An answer-choice may be incorrect because it doesn't properly answer the question or instead is missing something or contains something that is not in the content. You might ask the student, "How does this selection answer the question?" (with a focus on the question) or "Where is this answer in the content?" or "Is everything that is in the content also in this answer?" (with a focus back on the content).

There is no single one way to guide students to seeing that an answer-choice is incorrect. You will have to use your own skill in questioning to do so. But remember a few things.

- Try not to give students the answer. Generally speaking, they don't learn well from us just giving them the right answer.

- If you need to give the answer, say because class is about to end, do so and don't feel bad about it. There is always another day where you can use questions to lead them to understanding.

- Do not stick with one student for more than a few questions. If you keep working with one student only, the other students will start to tune out.

- Even if the student gives the correct response, without the justification component, it's almost like they just took a lucky guess.

Cognitive Roadblock: Elimination Strategy

The cognitive roadblock here is probably a consequence of the prominence of multiple-choice exams. It's when we ask students to eliminate an answer-choice as their first option rather than asking them to look for the correct answer first. It sort of goes like this:

Teacher: Okay, read all the answer-choices. Did you do that? Okay, which one of them can you eliminate?

If there are four answers available, and the student has eliminated one of them, then they now have three answer-choices left. If they haven't invested mental thought towards the correct answer, their odds of selecting the correct choice are one in three. Even when the student eliminates two answer-choices and has two left, if he hasn't focused on the correct answer, his odds are fifty-fifty. My point is, you can't eliminate your way to a correct answer. It does improve the odds but at some point the student has to focus on the right answer, not the several wrong ones.

So, start out by asking for correct answers. If the student makes a poor selection, work through it, eliminate it, and then ask again, "What is the best answer for this question?"

COMMON QUESTIONS

As you have been reading this book, I hope you sense that our approach to questioning is not set in stone. You may have to modify the strategies to fit your various classes and the needs of the students in them. One strategy may work well in one period but not in another. You should feel free to structure your questioning with what works for you.

There are several common questions that I am asked during workshops. I would like to review some of these questions below.

Q. I like to do Think-Pair-Share with students. Can I do that and still follow this model of questioning?

Absolutely! If you prefer to use a Think-Pair-Share approach rather than mostly calling on individual students, feel free to do so. There are advantages to calling on an individual student because you know exactly what that student knows. On the other hand, Think-Pair-Share may help make students more comfortable with participating because they share responsibility for creating a response and learn from each other. Both approaches are fine.

Q. Can I ask students to "pass the baton" and have each student select the next student who is to respond to a question?

Yes. If you want students to select who the next respondent is, please do so.

Q. Can I have students write out their responses rather than answer them orally?

Yes. I prefer an oral approach most of the time, but if the time seems right to have students write out their responses, you are at liberty to do so.

Q. I have lots of English-language learners in my class. How does the questioning work with them?

Any form of instruction where students are not fluent in the dominant language will be more challenging, regardless of whether you use questioning or lecture. You may have to translate questions or make the questions shorter or use more familiar verbs. Just remember that questioning still benefits the English-language learner. Imagine you take a trip to a foreign country and don't speak the language. If you stay in the hotel just listening to the TV, you probably will only pick up a little of the language. If you go out and engage the culture, you are much more likely to exercise the language out of necessity. Questioning is like going outside your hotel room and being forced to engage that world; lecture is more like listening to TV back in the hotel room.

Q. Can students ask questions to each other?

Yes. Once you make your students familiar with the cognitive levels of questioning and their order (i.e., steps), you may ask your students to pose questions to each other and observe the effects.

Q. Does it help to teach students the behavioral framework, rules like no "I don't know" beforehand?

Yes. It's a good idea to introduce your students to the expectations of questioning. That way, you don't surprise them.

Q. I like to ask an overview question to frame the lesson. Is that okay?

Yes. If it helps you to start the lesson with an overview question, which normally we might reserve until the middle or end of our questioning, you are free to do so.

Q. When do students get to ask questions to the teacher?

Whenever they want to!

Q. What if I really need to tell something to a student, may I do that?

Yes. If you feel you should tell a student something, please do so.

Q. It seems like this approach to questioning is very flexible and is more art than science?

I think that's just right. You must implement the strategies as you see fit with the knowledge that whatever you do, I've never heard of a student passing out from being asked a few questions!

CONCLUSION

Through your efforts in reading this book, I hope you have found some useful strategies that may help you ask questions to students more effectively. There is no single best way to ask students questions, but it is helpful to have some practical methods for encouraging participation or making sure that our questions actually lead to new moments of learning.

The recent epoch of the information revolution now brings a tremendous amount of content to our students. More than ever before in history, they have the opportunity to learn just about anything they want. But too many students remain unlikely to learn because they aren't motivated to do so or lack a reliable internal pattern for looking at information. Through our questioning strategies, I believe we can improve both things on both counts.

The main hurdle, then, really is in our own minds as teachers. I believe that students will adapt to almost any learning environment. As teachers, our culture has in some places become risk-averse. We may have become too hesitant to demand participation, speaking, and ultimately thinking, too.

There are many reasons to explain our reluctance to demand participation. But the time has come to have a discussion with parents and other educators about the nature of learning. As Dr. Feuerstein said, learning requires mediation. By their very nature, questioning strategies engender strong mediated learning experiences. These experiences are integral to developing critical thinking skills.

Also, as Americans, our Constitution demands an inquisitive citizenry. The Constitution doesn't protect us from malefactors like a token or amulet of protection. A generation dulled from inquiry may end up with less freedom than the preceding generation simply because, by their temperament, they allowed their freedoms to be slowly diminished. Questions are at the heart of a strong country, I believe.

I wish you good luck in trying out the strategies you have learned in this book and remain open to your input and feedback about the strategies themselves. I do not think the book is closed on how to ask questions in the classroom. I remain open to questions about questioning, so to speak.

Thank you for your efforts to learn and for creating learning in your students. And please contact me as desired for workshops or other information.

Sincerely,

Ivan Hannel

ivan@apoq.org

ABOUT THE AUTHOR

Gerardo Ivan Hannel was born in 1971 in Nashville, Tennessee. He grew up in Phoenix and went to college at Yale University and law school at Northwestern University School of Law. He has given teacher-training workshops in questioning strategies since 1995. He is currently a practicing trial attorney in civil litigation in Phoenix, Arizona. He is available by email to ivan@apoq.org or 602-710-7573.

Made in the USA
Columbia, SC
20 April 2021